TRAVEL HACKS

An Hachette UK Company
www.hachette.co.uk

Summersdale Publishers Ltd
Part of Octopus Publishing Group Limited
Carmelite House
50 Victoria Embankment
LONDON
EC4Y 0DZ
UK

www.summersdale.com

Printed and bound in Croatia

ISBN: 978-1-78685-271-7

Substantial discounts on bulk quantities of Summersdale books are available to corporations, professional associations and other organisations. For details contact general enquiries: telephone: +44 (0) 1243 771107 or email: enquiries@summersdale.com.

TRAVEL HACKS

Tips and Tricks for Happier Trips

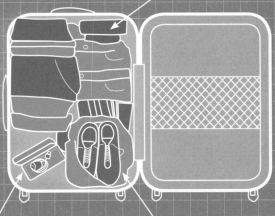

Rolled-up clothes for extra space

Tangle-free and tidy leads

Shower-cap dirt-catcher

Dan Marshall

Over **120** amazing hacks inside!

summersdale

DISCLAIMER

Neither the author nor the publisher can be held responsible for any loss or claim arising out of the use, or misuse, of the suggestions made herein.

CONTENTS

INTRODUCTION

In the age of budget airlines that fly across the globe and smartphones that can provide detailed offline maps, book taxis, restaurants and hotels, as well as take 'artistic' photos with just a few clicks, you might think you've got it pretty good when it comes to travelling. But where's the app to stop your toiletries from leaking all over your best Hawaiian shirt, or to save that extra bit of space in your suitcase for your beloved unicorn slippers? Don't bother googling it, those apps don't exist. You've got *Travel Hacks* now so everything is going to be OK.

This book will give you practical hints and tips for all kinds of excursions and accommodation, from beach holidays to camping trips, and from the most humble of hotel rooms to the front seat of your car. Armed with this book, you can set off and head for any horizon you fancy, safe in the knowledge that you'll be able to navigate without the aid of the internet, clear water from your ears and protect your precious food store from marauding wildlife, all in the time it takes you to turn a few pages. *Bon voyage*!

BOOKING HACKS

All journeys start with a single step – but sometimes that single step isn't a simple one. This chapter will show you how to overcome the online obstacles that can appear even before you've decided which swimsuit to wear, ensuring that you'll get the best price on your travel and accommodation.

INSIDER INFO

Unless you're a Knight of the Round Table, you're probably not a fan of spam. But there is such a thing as 'good' spam when it comes to getting advance information on cheap flights.

Simply signing up to an airline's mailing list will actually generate useful emails detailing special offers and bonus air-mile promotions. So, instead of information about bulk deals on protein shakes or the hot new colours for this season's wall paint, your inbox will be full of travel goodness.

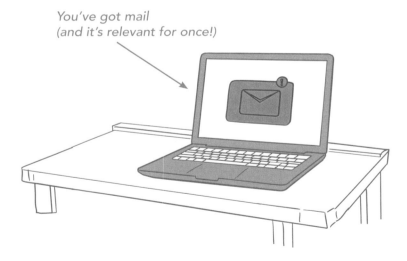

You've got mail (and it's relevant for once!)

THE EARLY BOOKER CATCHES THE WORM

When it comes to travel arrangements, leaving things to the last minute is not always advisable. You might be tempted by a 'late deal' scenario, but nothing beats the smug satisfaction of having locked that flight date into your calendar – especially if you want to post annoying updates on social media about how many 'sleeps' you have left.

Booking flights in the first four months of the year – and at least 47–53 days before you wish to depart – will usually give you the cheapest price.

Flight booked in the first four months of the year

You

FLY FLEXI

For most people, having to change travel plans is a serious pain. Whether you're taking the trip of a lifetime or just looking forward to your annual family break, the last thing you want is a spanner in the works. But there is a way to dodge this bullet and potentially save money.

By booking with airlines that provide flexible fares you can reserve a seat on your chosen date and later change that date should you need to, which means that you can potentially book off-peak and – provided the dates are available – fly peak. Especially useful in a school summer holiday scenario. Some companies will offer free hold luggage and early boarding with this option too, but offers vary so be sure to read the Ts and Cs.

The priciest month of the year just got cheaper

ONE-WAY VAYCAY

You would think that committing to travel to and from your destination with the same company would get you a better deal on your ticket - customer loyalty and all that - but that's not always the case.

It might actually be cheaper to buy two low-priced one-way tickets, usually with different airlines, rather than a round-trip ticket. The same can also apply to train journeys, so shop around!

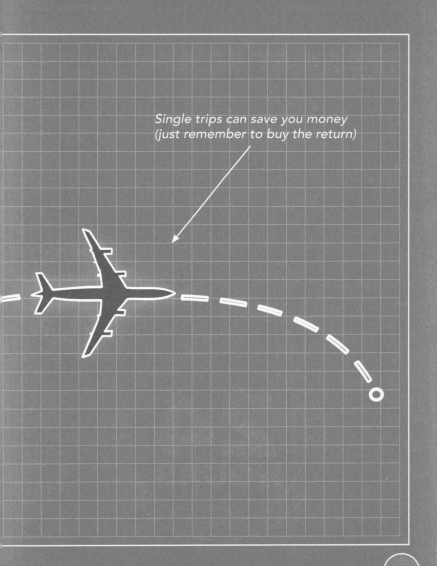

Single trips can save you money
(just remember to buy the return)

THE 24-HOUR RULE

Even if you've been hack-smart and got your early-bird fare locked in (see page 10), there might still be a way to save even more of your hard-earned cash.

Many airlines allow travellers to cancel tickets within 24 hours of booking without a fee. You should always read the small print, but it's worth a final check after booking your flight: a better price or flash airfare sale might have popped up!

The 24-hour clock is ticking

REFUND REQUEST

Nobody enjoys finding out they could have paid less for something. Even though the money's gone and you've probably forgotten all about it, finding out that somebody else paid less is aggravating. But don't break out the punchbag just yet.

If you book a flight and then find out that by some miracle the prices have since gone down, ask the company to refund the difference. It might not always work, as all airlines have different policies, but it wouldn't do you any harm to ask.

The look of shock when you find out you could have paid less for your holiday

PLUS ONE

To most regular-thinking folks, the fewer days you spend on holiday, the less it will cost. A logical argument in my eyes. However, many accommodation companies are one step ahead and know that they can put the prices up for this type of short getaway routine. So, if you're able to turn that weekend trip into a long-weekend stay or turn a week into an odd-sounding eight days of escape, try it and perhaps you'll beat them at their own game.

If it helps, use a spreadsheet just like this one to compare the costs

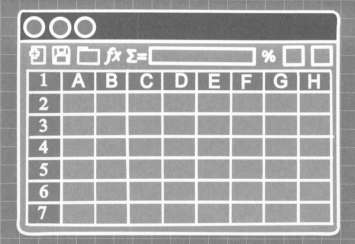

DRIVING FOR A BARGAIN

So you've decided to hire a car while you're on holiday? How very brave of you! I'd recommend a tank; it will save you having to learn how to drive on the wrong side of the road – you'll be driving on both.

If you'd rather get a hire car, the trick is to book it as early as possible before you travel. It can be as cheap as £6 a day (excluding extras like insurance), which is worth booking in preparation, rather than having to pay 10 times that amount when you arrive.

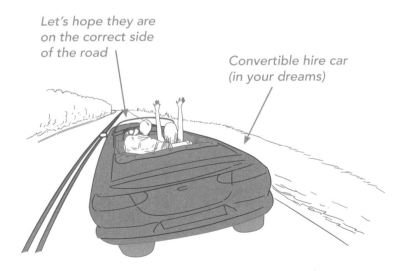

Let's hope they are on the correct side of the road

Convertible hire car (in your dreams)

PACKING HACKS

Ah, the age-old battle of wits – traveller vs suitcase. Technically, you have the upper hand, what with your case being an unthinking, inanimate object of regular shape and size, but you should never underestimate your opponent. You know that sucker can have you tearing your hair out and rolling around the floor in a fit of rage. This chapter will make packing a breeze.

FILL YOUR BOOTS

When it comes to taking up space in your bag or suitcase, shoes are often right up there as the worst offenders. They're heavy, bulky and possibly stinky. But you can take advantage of this (except for the smell) with this hack.

Stuff smaller items like underwear, socks or chargers into the shoes to make use of all of that empty space. That way, they don't just have a 'sole purpose'.

Perfectly packed suitcase

Filled with socks all
the way to the toe

DON'T DOUBLE UP

Here's another no-brainer (yet it's surprising how many people don't think of it). If a hairdryer is essential to your morning routine you might be planning on taking one in your suitcase. However, if the place you're staying in can provide one you're just weighing yourself down!

Take the time to research what facilities your room/hotel offers *before* you start packing. Email them directly if you have to. It will save you the effort of putting your back out carrying an over-packed case.

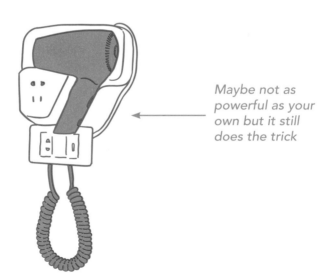

Maybe not as powerful as your own but it still does the trick

MULTIPURPOSE CLOTHES

Over-packing is a pretty easy trap to fall into. You want to be prepared for all conditions and situations – and how could you leave your lucky poncho behind?! Much like your shoes (see page 20), many items of clothing have alternative uses that make packing more efficient.

If you're going to be travelling on buses a lot a jumper could be used as a pillow; if you're heading somewhere hot, a sarong can work as a headscarf or a light blanket. While flying or on the move, you can wear your most bulky, heavy or hard-to-pack items to save space and the unexpected surcharge for overweight luggage. Just don't get too excited and put on too many layers – you need to be able to fit through the plane door!

Jumpers-cum-comfy headrest

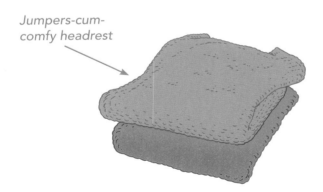

THE BURRITO ROLL

Do you like burritos? Well, sadly, this hack is not a recipe, but it is a tasty offering in terms of space-saving. Everyone needs to pack essentials, such as underwear and socks, but not everyone does it properly. Here's how the experts do it.

Take a vest/T-shirt and lay it out on a flat surface. Place a pair of pants, shorts or a skirt in the chest area and fold the arms of the shirt towards the middle. Place a pair of ankle-length socks horizontally at the top of the shirt, open ends facing outwards, and roll the shirt tightly up. To seal the burrito, turn the ends of the socks over the whole roll.

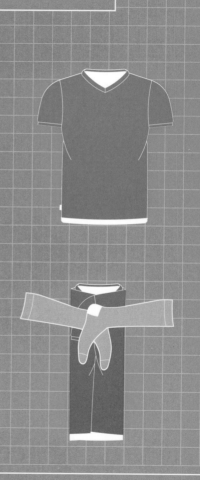

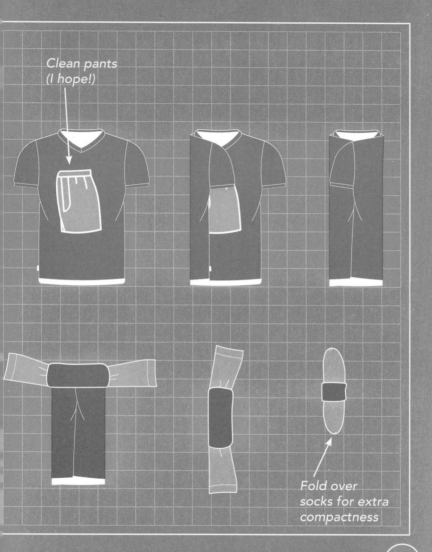

Clean pants
(I hope!)

Fold over
socks for extra
compactness

25

LEAK-FREE BOTTLES

The last thing you want to see when opening your bag or suitcase is a cocktail of shampoo, toothpaste and shower gel slowly soaking into your diamante-encrusted bathing suit. Here's how to prevent such a disaster.

Simply cut out a small square of cling film, unscrew the lid of the potentially leaky product, put the cling film on top and screw the lid back on. Repeat for all of your toiletries.

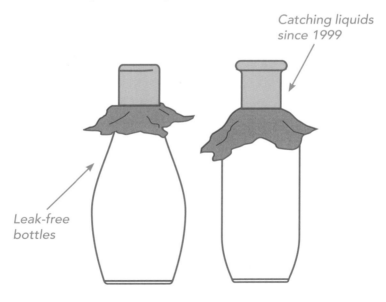

Catching liquids since 1999

Leak-free bottles

SHOE DIAPERS

Have you ever actually used one of those weird plastic shower caps you find in hotels? If the answer is yes, the chances are you have somehow travelled back in time to the 1980s. If, like most people, you look at them in bemusement, here's a hack that can show you what to do with them.

If your shoes are soiled from all that holiday walking, slip them inside the novelty shower cap before placing them in your bag. That way your clothes will stay clean during transit!

Whatever you do, don't forget to take these off before going out in public!

STRUCTURAL PACKING

If looking sharp is high on your holiday agenda, you need a way of packing your bag without squashing your clothes into a wrinkled heap. Here are a few hacks to keep you looking fly.

To ensure your shirt collar stays straight, try rolling up a belt and slotting it into the neck as a support. To keep that ridiculous straw hat you already regret buying at least modestly in shape, fold a small towel or T-shirt and put it inside the hat to keep it from getting flattened in transit.

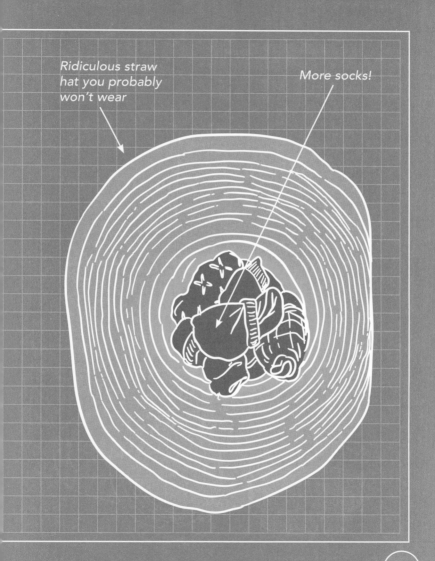

Ridiculous straw hat you probably won't wear

More socks!

CONVENIENT CONTAINERS

With restrictions on transporting liquids and gels in hand luggage, you might find yourself struggling to cover the essentials. Don't buy overpriced 'travel size' toiletries – just make your own with some small containers!

Contact lens cases and empty prescription bottles are airtight and can be sealed easily. Just decant your liquids and gels into them. If you don't have any of those things, nip down to your local pharmacy – many now sell mini containers of all shapes and sizes for this purpose – and they're reusable!

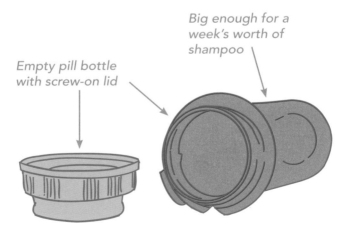

Big enough for a week's worth of shampoo

Empty pill bottle with screw-on lid

TRINKET TRANSPORTATION 1

If you've ever tried to transport jewellery in your bag before (especially necklaces and bracelets) you'll know that most likely they end up in knots so complex you need a magnifying glass and some tweezers to unravel them. Here's how to avoid the tangles and the turmoil.

Take an old pill organiser and use it to keep smaller items like rings and earrings together. For necklaces and bracelets, grab some drinking straws. Thread half of the chain through the straw (cut one down for your bracelets) and do up the clasp in order to arrive at your destination knot free!

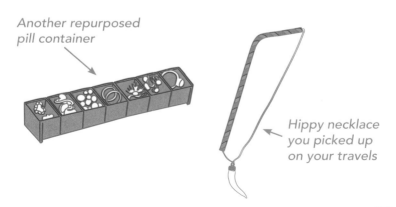

Another repurposed pill container

Hippy necklace you picked up on your travels

RAZOR HOLSTER

If you're a fan of cheap, disposable razors, you'll know that it's pretty easy to cut yourself while shaving! The same goes for when you're transporting them in your bag while travelling. If they're knocking about and the plastic guard has come off, they might well do some damage.

So avoid this mishap and sheath them quickly and easily with a foldback clip. Clip it over the business end of your razor and rest assured the blade will be safe. (The clip can then be used to keep your important documents together once you arrive at your destination!)

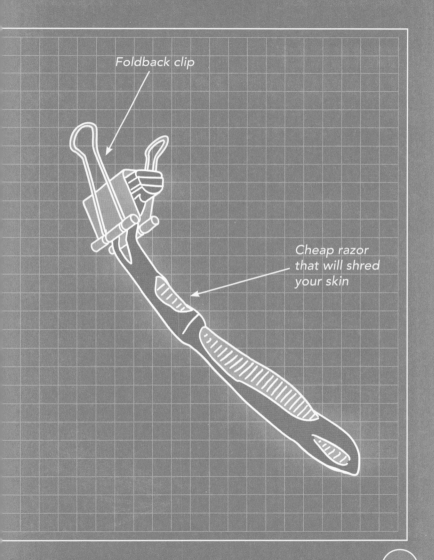

Foldback clip

Cheap razor
that will shred
your skin

33

TRINKET TRANSPORTATION 2

If you travel with so many trinkets that you need even more packing inspiration, here's another handy tip to keep those easily misplaced items safe.

Use an empty Tic Tac container – or an old-fashioned mint tin, if you can find one – to keep your small, loose items together. A tin is ideal for lip balm, phone-charging leads and loose change; use your Tic Tac box for things like hairgrips.

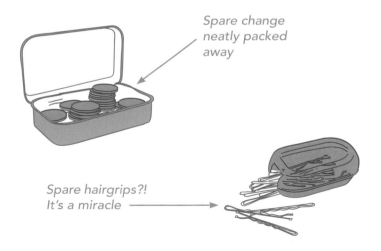

Spare change neatly packed away

Spare hairgrips?! It's a miracle

GADGET ESSENTIALS CARRYCASE

Much like your jewellery (see page 31), gadget leads and headphone cords can get into a horrific tangle when in transit. And nobody needs to experience the lightning strike of panic when you can't find your phone charger in your bag, even though you were sure you put it in there.

Save the hassle by placing your loose cords, earphones and chargers into an old sunglasses case. They'll be safe and you'll know exactly where they are when you search for them in your carry-on bag or unpack your suitcase!

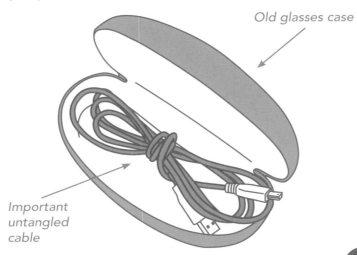

Old glasses case

Important untangled cable

MIX-AND-MATCH PACKING

Although packing a change of clothes in your carry-on luggage (neatly packed in your burrito roll, see page 24) is a great idea, hold luggage, funnily enough, is more out of your hands. When travelling in a pair or checking in more than one suitcase, consider swapping some complete outfits or essentials between bags so that if one gets lost or delayed, you'll have backups. Once all your luggage is safely retrieved, you can return clothes to their rightful owners – or create some crazy mix-and-match get-ups!

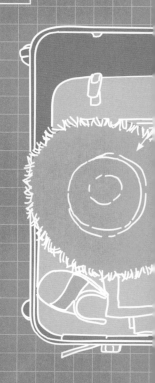

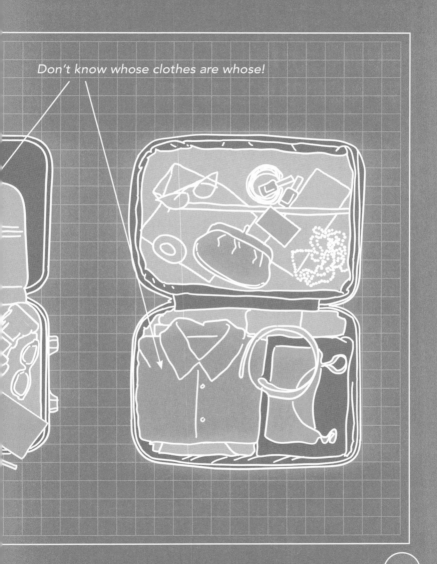

Don't know whose clothes are whose!

SUITCASE SPACE MAXIMISER

An industrial amount of holiday clothes needs an industrial-style packing solution. Here's how to get an obscene amount into your bag or case.

Invest in some vacuum storage bags. As well as being handy for use at home, less dense items such as fluffy jumpers and socks can be squished down to a fraction of their size for packing! This will also provide bonus waterproofing against those leaky toiletries (that is, if you haven't used the hack on page 26). But remember – this won't make your clothes weigh any less, so be sure to check how heavy your bag is afterwards. When packing to go home, make sure you have access to a vacuum cleaner otherwise your clothes may not fit back in your suitcase.

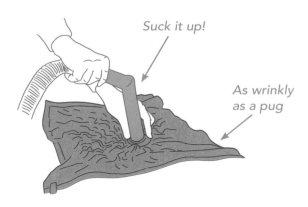

Suck it up!

As wrinkly as a pug

PRE-FLIGHT HACKS

Getting a good price for your flight is pretty easy now that there are a million price-comparison websites to do the work for you. But what about protecting your luggage from inconsiderate baggage handlers, getting your precious souvenirs home without hassle and being prepared when you've mislaid your passport? Read on!

HANDLE WITH CARE

Have you ever collected your luggage at the airport and found it in such a state that it looks like someone has dropped it off the top of a building and then jumped up and down on it a couple of times for good measure?

It goes without saying that anything fragile should be taken to the appropriate baggage area, but if you're concerned about your bag being treated roughly, mark it as 'FRAGILE' anyway, to ensure it's handled with care.

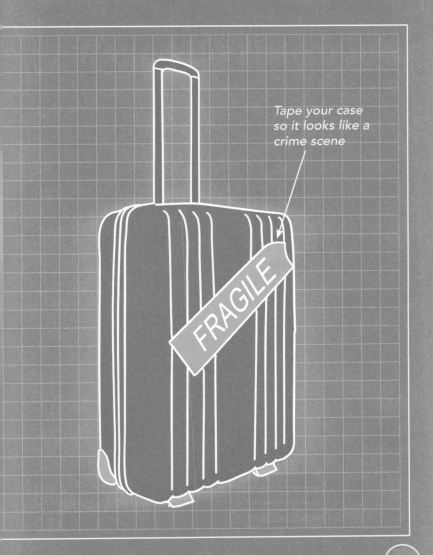

Tape your case so it looks like a crime scene

FRAGILE

DOCUMENT DUPLICATES

Ever been abroad and thought you'd lost your passport? It's heart-attack scary. What makes a few pieces of paper so important?! Well, they are, so you have to live with it.

You can save yourself the worry of the prospect of losing this and all of your other important bits of paper by simply making a copy of them for when you travel. You could even save an electronic copy to your phone and/or email them to yourself so you have a virtual record. A screenshot of your passport won't be valid for travel, but having all of your passport details to hand will be invaluable if it does go AWOL.

Definitely not the work printer…

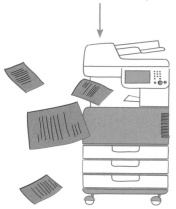

Fake passport

SMART SEATING

Do you hate being cramped in your budget airline seat? Well, then you should save up for a better seat, you cheapskate! But if that's not an option, consider gaining some extra room by being tactical about your reservations.

When booking seats for two people, choose the aisle and window seats. Chances are no one will take the middle seat, and you can spread yourselves luxuriously across the full row. If someone does take that middle seat, just ask them to switch so you can sit with your travel companion, and hope that they're kind enough to agree.

You   _Stranger_   _Travel buddy_

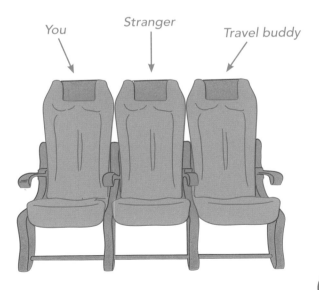

BUDGET BREKKIE

If you're not a fan of the ludicrous prices charged for even the most basic of snacks on so-called budget airlines, this one's for you.

For a cheaper (and possibly healthier) in-flight breakfast, transfer a packet of instant oatmeal into a reusable cup with a lid, along with your favourite toppings, such as dried fruit, nuts or chocolate chips, before you fly. When you're peckish, break it out and just ask for hot water!

The breakfast of
travel-hack champions

SLEEP TIGHT AND EAT RIGHT

Jet lag is a major drag, but there's no need to fall victim to this time-zone-induced madness!

Minimise your pain by loading up on sleep a week before you head off on your travels. You can also start to shift your meals and bedtime closer to the hours that you'll experience at your destination. Go to bed and get up an hour earlier than usual before heading east, and do the same, but one hour later than usual, before heading west. Try to avoid alcohol, caffeine and heavily processed foods before and during your flight, as these will only work to upset your stomach and therefore your sleep.

This hack doesn't encourage eating clocks

BUDGET-BEATING HACKS

Everyone loves a bargain! And I'm guessing, since you bought a book on travel hacks, you'd benefit from a few shortcuts. This chapter is full of general-purpose advice on how to save money while travelling, from stocking up on essentials to saving yourself money when purchasing foreign currency.

KNOW YOUR CUSTOMS

When planning to visit a foreign country you will no doubt do some kind of research. For most people this will involve choosing accommodation, maybe selecting a few choice activities and perhaps some places you might eat. This is all good, but spare a moment to consider doing a bit of research on the culture too.

It might be there are certain customs that are widely accepted throughout the country you are visiting, and not being in the know could lead to both embarrassment and extra wallet damage. For instance, in Spain, it is generally accepted that table water is to be paid for and will automatically be brought out for you. In China, it is customary for a host to never let a teacup go empty, so refills will keep happening as long as you're finishing your drink. Be sure to do your research so you have money left over to spend on those essential souvenirs.

The unamused expression one makes on finding out that tap water isn't free

49

THE 'BURBS

Far from being full of crazed weirdos who may or may not be disposing of bodies in their basement, the suburbs have lots to offer the intrepid traveller.

The main advantage of getting out of the tourist hotspots while visiting a new place is that most things you buy will be cheaper. Secondly, you will be experiencing a more local culture, uncompromised by the desire to cash in on prospective tourists' cash. A great way to find out more is to check websites such as Like a Local (likealocalguide.com) or message boards on Lonely Planet or TripAdvisor.

Nondescript
suburban setting

Lapping up the
local culture

CASH-SAVVY

Most people will think to purchase their foreign currency well ahead of their trip. It's part of the preparation process and there's nothing wrong with that. However, if you hold out until you arrive at your destination you can make a tidy saving.

If you draw money out of an ATM in the country of your destination, you can avoid losing out due to high conversion rates. But be sure to accept the ATM's option to pay in the local currency and only withdraw large sums of money at once to maximise savings. If you want to make multiple small transactions, use your credit card for this. Alternatively, services like Caxton and Revolut currency cards allow you to transfer and withdraw money from bank machines without fees attached. Do your research and find a card free from fees.

Don't be fooled – it's your turn next

BUDGET TV BINGE

This hack is for those who subscribe to the popular on-demand TV service that ends in 'flix'. If you're going to be travelling for a long time or confine yourself to your room because you actually hate holidays, there's a way to make your viewing experience less data-hungry.

To do this, change your playback settings. Log in via a browser (not the app) and go to 'account settings', then switch playback from 'auto' to 'low'. This means you'll be using less data and it's also perfect for weaker Wi-Fi connections. Alternatively, you can download programmes before you go to watch while travelling or when in places with no internet.

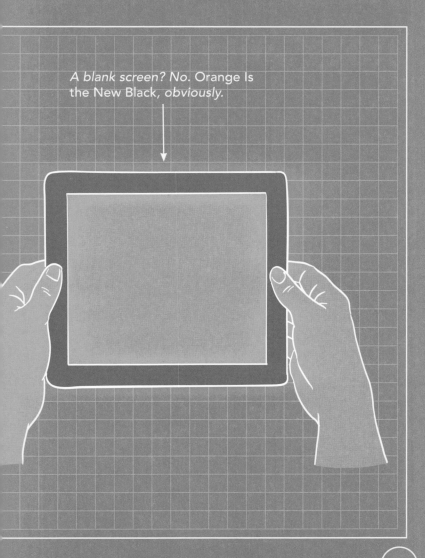

A *blank screen*? No. Orange Is the New Black, *obviously.*

SNACK STOCK-UP

The simplest ideas are sometimes so obvious people miss them altogether. This hack is one of those. At some point on your holiday you'll be hungry for a snack and of course you'll want a drink too.

Even if your hotel has the most tempting room-service menu you've ever seen, you'll be far better off getting some basic snacks and drinks for your room from a local store. It will be cheaper and you might even find some local delicacies that aren't available at your hotel!

Cheap food means you can buy double the amount!

HELLO H₂O

Keeping yourself hydrated when travelling is essential – but if you're buying from anywhere vaguely touristy – including the airport – you're going to be paying over the odds.

A better way is to either invest in a durable water flask, or remember to pack an empty plastic bottle before you leave. That way, you can use free water sources – like airport fountains (maybe not airport toilets!), as well as public sources like cafes, restaurants and hotels. You won't get that mineral-filtered taste, but who cares? It's water!

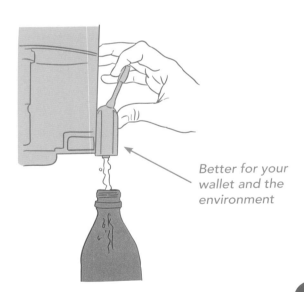

Better for your wallet and the environment

HACKS ON THE GO

A big part of travelling is, well, travelling. That is, getting from A to B in some form of transport. Many people enjoy the build-up, experience and aftermath of being in transit (and why wouldn't you, if you're travelling first class?!), but if the thought of interminable car journeys and joyless flights fills you with mild panic, this chapter is for you.

HOME-MADE MOBILE SPEAKER

Want to rock out to some classic travel tunes but don't have any sort of speakers for your phone? This hack will show you how!

Simply take a finished toilet roll tube (or extract a new one, if you're really keen) and cut a phone-sized slit in the side of it. Insert the phone, select 'hair metal playlist' and you're rockin'! If you don't have a toilet roll handy, just pop your phone into a cup or anything else vaguely cylindrical for a similar effect.

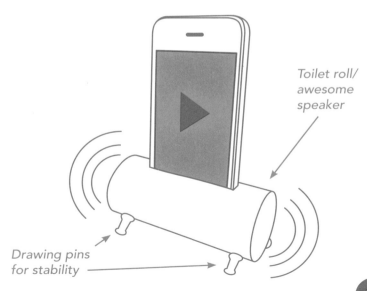

Toilet roll/ awesome speaker

Drawing pins for stability

CEREAL KILLER

If you're on the road for a long period of time, you're bound to get hungry. Whether you break out the boiled sweets or the 2-foot submarine sandwich, you're going to be generating rubbish. We've all stashed chocolate bar wrappers in the door compartment in our cars, but here's a hack to show you that there's no need.

Use an empty cereal container lodged in the footwell as a mini rubbish bin, lined with a plastic or paper bag for easy disposal, keeping your car litter-free!

Once full, just remove the lid, take out the bag and dispose of it in a bin

BACK-SEAT BLOW-UP BED

Ever tried to spend the night sleeping in a car while on a marathon road trip? You can guarantee dribble and neck-ache will be involved! Unless you use this hack, that is.

If there's a chance you'll be doing a lot of miles in your motor, pack an inflatable lilo. If you're opting for a car kip, pump that sucker up and lay it across the back seat for something vaguely comfortable. NB – this will not work if you own a Fiat 500 or anything similarly bijou.

Your comfy, albeit slightly snug, sleeping quarters for the night

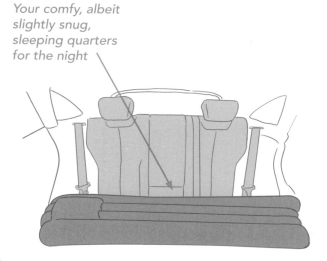

CAR CADDIES

If your car is woefully short of handy holders and places to stash little travel essentials for long journeys in the family car here's a solution for you.

Try attaching shower caddies with suction cups to the back windows of the car and fill them with games, snacks and anything else your passengers may want handy. Just be sure to leave some room at the bottom of the window to roll it down – if you don't, the cups will hit the door sill and be knocked off, leaving your precious travel sweets scattered all over the floor!

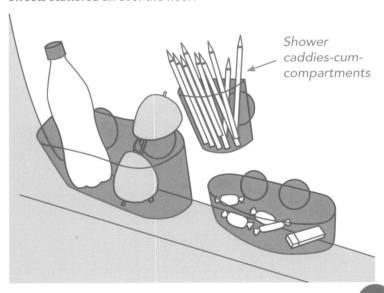

Shower caddies-cum-compartments

SNOOZE AND (DON'T) LOSE

What's more innocent than pulling over for a refreshing nap when on a long car journey? After all, tiredness kills. Follow these tips to snooze worry-free.

The first thing to consider when taking an in-car nap is safety. If you're out in the sticks, try using an app to locate a free camping spot. If not, try to find somewhere that isn't too remote and be sure to lock your doors before you turn out the lights.

Ensure you sleep in the passenger or back seat. In some areas of the US, for instance, you risk being fined when snoozing in the driver's seat.

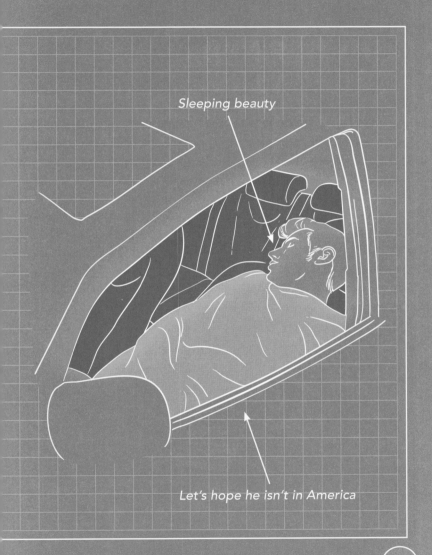

CAR FRESHENER

Small, confined spaces, like cars, tend to trap bad odours. Yes, you can crack open a window, but not when it's freezing outside, and not when travelling at high speeds (unless you fancy an impromptu blow-dry and ear-blasting). Add food to the mix and your car travels are going to get funky – and we're not talking James Brown.

To combat the pong, tape a tumble dryer sheet partially over an air vent to help dispel unwanted smells. It's just a mask for the smell, sure, but it will make the journey more bearable!

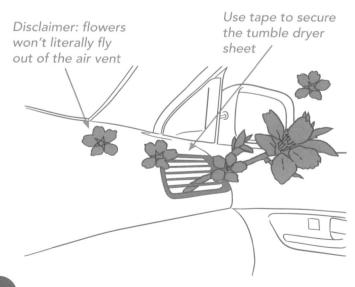

Disclaimer: flowers won't literally fly out of the air vent

Use tape to secure the tumble dryer sheet

IN-FLIGHT SMARTPHONE TV

If you're on an endless journey on a bus or a plane and you're not lucky enough to have seat-back TVs, fret not. There's a simple solution that will keep you (and your tribe) happy.

Put your phone in a clear plastic bag and attach it to the seat in front of you. Then sit back and relax. Your in-flight viewing system is ready! Just remember to cut a hole so you can plug in some headphones – not everybody will want to listen to *Peppa Pig*.

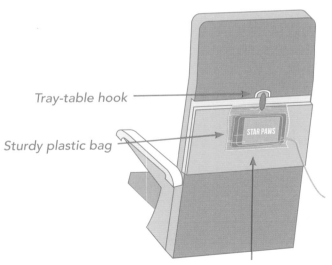

Tray-table hook

STAR PAWS

Sturdy plastic bag

Movie-playing device

WE GOT OURSELVES A CONVOY!

Chances are you won't be driving a big rig and Burt Reynolds will not be in attendance, but if you plan to drive en masse on a motorway this hack will help.

There's a trick to keeping your crew together. When changing lane, the leading car should indicate, then the second and third car in succession. The third car can then move over, followed by the second and then the first. This way, no one gets left behind and the first driver needn't wait, trying to judge if a gap is big enough for the whole line. Ten-four!

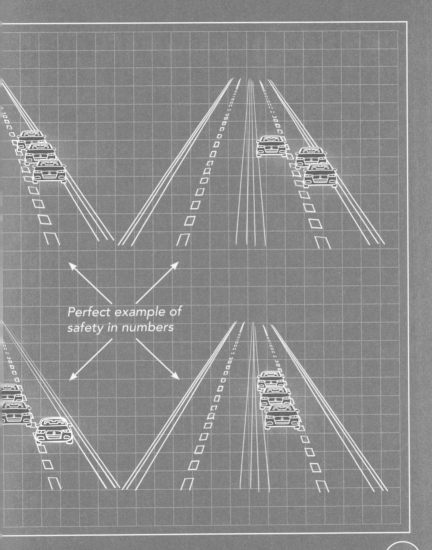

*Perfect example of
safety in numbers*

CUP-HOLDER ORGANISER

Remember when cup holders in cars were a radical new invention? No, I don't either. Lots of cars have them now, but chances are you don't use them for holding drinks. You probably use them for storing tat – loose change, batteries, chewing gum. All of which becomes impossible to fish out again, because the holders are so narrow and, you know, made for cups. But here's a way of making them function better.

Line the bottom of your cup holders with cupcake cases. That way, you can grab the edge of the case and easily lift out your tiny travel essentials all at once.

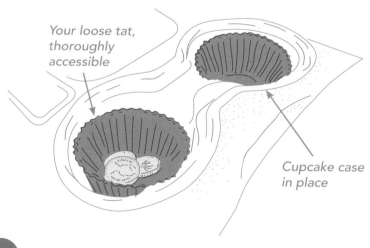

Your loose tat, thoroughly accessible

Cupcake case in place

SPILL-FREE DRINKING

Attempting to drink from a cup in a moving vehicle is challenging on the best of days, let alone when you have a driver who seems to veer inexplicably towards potholes. So when kids are involved, you better believe there's going to be spillage. Unless you use this ingenious hack.

If they're desperate for a drink and you're using a cup, fill it, then cover the opening with cling film and pierce it with a straw. You now have a makeshift, no-spill drinking vessel.

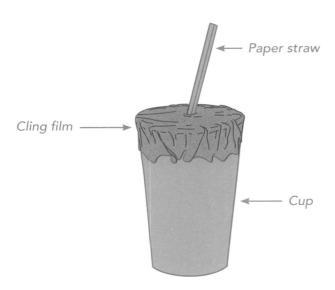

← Paper straw

Cling film →

← Cup

BACK-SEAT BAG HANGER

Do you own an expensive designer handbag or a much-loved novelty umbrella that you are loath to simply dump in the dirty footwell when you have a car full of passengers or the hire car floor looks suspiciously sticky? You're not alone.

Don't settle for degrading your stuff, create a quick and easy way of stowing it above the danger zone by simply adding a carabiner or two to the stem(s) of your headrest. From this you can hang your precious items. No more scuffs on my Hello Kitty merch!

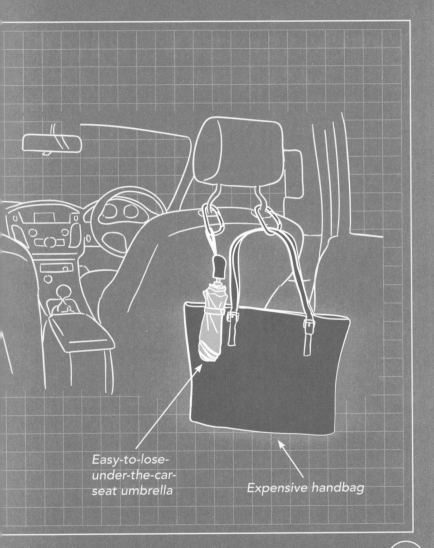

Easy-to-lose-under-the-car-seat umbrella

Expensive handbag

QUICK GUIDE TO JUMP-STARTING

Here's a trick every vehicle owner should know how to execute (and one of the few things you don't need the official garage mechanic to do). When your battery is flat and you're stuck, the temptation is to call for roadside assistance, but if you're in a residential area it could well be quicker to ask a kindly stranger to give you a jump-start. For those who know, here's a reminder. For those who don't – you're welcome. (Plus, now you know you can repay the favour and help someone else out.)

1. Red on dead positive
2. Red on donor positive
3. Black on donor negative
4. Black on something metal of the dead car (such as the bonnet)
5. Start the donor, then start the dead and remove leads in 4, 3, 2, 1.

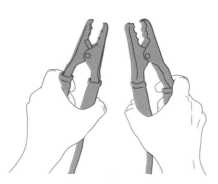

ROAD RULES

Using the road in a foreign country can be daunting to say the least. Chances are you'll be a bit less confident than usual and the experience will only be made worse by not knowing the rules of the road.

So wise up before you get behind the wheel. Don't just check the speed limits, but also the amount of alcohol you can drink before driving and the insurance needed too. You might also find it handy to look at how the climate of another place can affect a vehicle and general driving – do you need snow chains to get to the local *boulangerie*? All stuff you need to know!

*Lifting the bonnet
just because...*

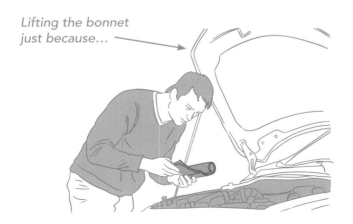

EMERGENCY SICK KIT

Travelling with the smell of vomit in your vicinity is the stuff of nightmares. So whether you suffer from travel sickness or have a car full of chunder-prone rugrats, you need to be prepared for the worst.

So carry a 'sick kit'. The key items to include would be: travel-sickness tablets, sick bags, mints, tissues and wipes, anti-bacterial hand gel, a towel to cover whoever feels sick (to avoid the car and themselves becoming sick central), bottles of water for cleaning and drinking, and small snacks to fill an empty stomach to reduce the chance of more sickness.

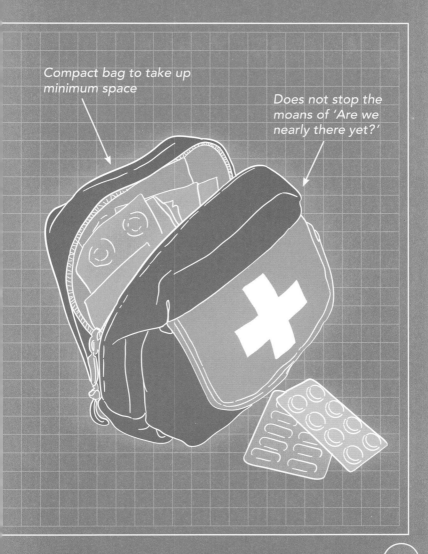

Compact bag to take up minimum space

Does not stop the moans of 'Are we nearly there yet?'

BE SOLAR-SAVVY

A long journey in a car, or on a bus or train, equals long bouts of boredom for passengers, which is where smartphones and tablets come in. But what if the power runs out?

Well, you can be smart and arm yourself with solar chargers. These babies stick to the window and use the sun's rays to create energy for your boredom-busting gadgets. So you'll be able to keep yourself, or your passengers, screen-ready for the whole journey.

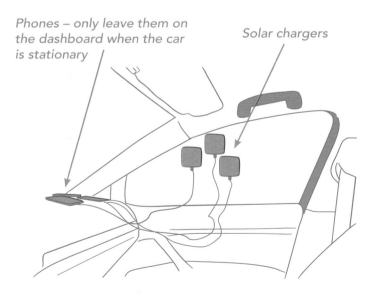

Phones – only leave them on the dashboard when the car is stationary

Solar chargers

ACCOMMODATION HACKS

What good is a journey without a destination? Especially if that destination features an exquisite king-size bed and Jacuzzi bath. But chances are, unless you are spending big bucks – and, let's face it, if you are you don't need hacks, you have money! – you're not heading for such a place. So when your bog-standard room is giving you the blues, you can call upon the hacks in this chapter to save the day.

TICKET TO RIDE

If you're in a foreign country and you can't speak the language (and the locals are not inclined to speak your native tongue) you're going to hit a communication wall at some point. Getting pigs' trotters instead of pizza is one thing, but not being able to tell your taxi driver where they are taking you back to is a disaster.

Avoid this by seeking out the business card for your accommodation and putting it in your wallet. Most if not all business cards will have an address on, so if your driver is looking at you blankly you can simply show them the card and you'll be on your way. (Take a sheet of addressed notepaper from your room if no cards are available.)

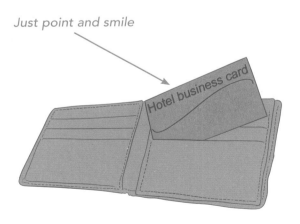

Just point and smile

BODY LOTION BUFFER

When you're on holiday, one of the last things you'll be thinking about is shoe polish. But if you're dining out in some swanky restaurant – perhaps it's your anniversary or you just like looking super fly – and your shoes are a mess, you need a solution.

Look no further than your complimentary hotel toiletries. With luck you'll spot a bottle of body lotion which, amazing but true, will double up as shoe polish. Rub it in with a bit of tissue, and then buff with a clean piece to achieve a gleam you can see your own reflection in (and sweet-scented shoes to boot!).

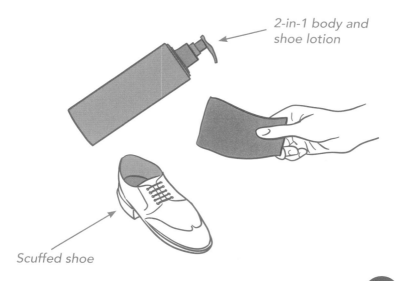

2-in-1 body and shoe lotion

Scuffed shoe

EXTRA JUICE

Like many smartphone and tablet users, you might have developed something of a screen habit. So once you've arrived at your accommodation, you'll probably be well up for a phone session – except, your battery is almost dead and, when you check your bag, you've forgotten your universal plug adapter (insert blood-curdling scream sound effect here).

But don't have a heart attack just yet. You can charge devices without a plug through the USB slot of a TV, presuming your room has one. Just check the back for the port and charge away.

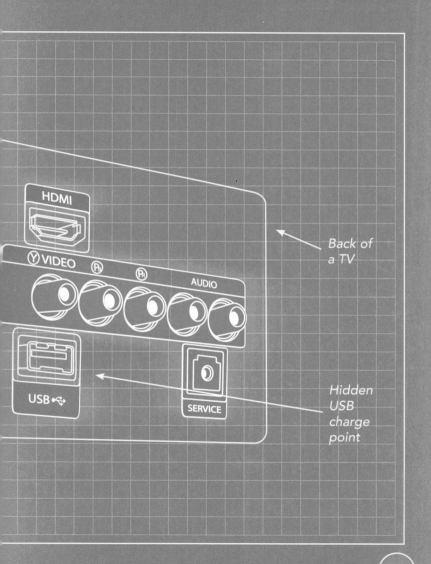

HDMI

Y VIDEO   Pʙ   Pʀ   AUDIO

USB

SERVICE

Back of a TV

Hidden USB charge point

81

CHECK THIS

Checking into a hotel is always a pain. Sure, maybe you've been lucky and the staff are pleasant, but it's such an unnecessary song and dance. That is, unless they're singing to your tune.

If you purposely check in at the later end of the window, and your hotel is the sort that allocates rooms to guests as they arrive, you might be in for a win. Chances are that by the time you get to the hotel to check in, all the standard rooms will have gone and you'll have a shot at being given a free upgrade!

A fashionably late check-in

Put on your best smile ⟶

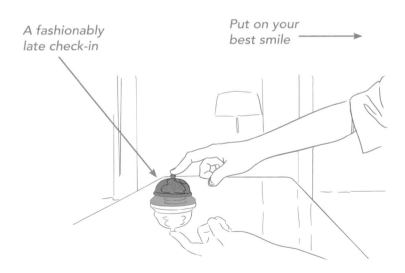

PILLOW PLUMP

If you're like me and you value sleep pretty much above all else in life (or at least on an equal footing with food), you'll always be a little sceptical when it comes to your hotel bed. There are so many areas which could let it down, but not many you can actually do something about. But here's one you can.

If your pillow is too soft, beef it up by stuffing the case (preferably on the underside) with a spare towel. The result will be a firmer, comfier pillow and hopefully a more restful night.

How many towels does it take to plump a pillow?

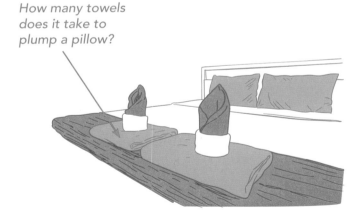

MATTRESS MAGIC

Now that you've got your pillow sorted (see page 83), check out your mattress. This is a little trickier, as it's such a big area and a little more complex than a bag full of feathers, but you can still hack your way to a better bed.

If your mattress is sagging in places, bolster it underneath with the extra pillows and blankets that are hopefully lurking in your wardrobe. If the mattress seems too hard, ask at reception for a duvet, which any good hotel should be able to provide, and lay it underneath the sheet.

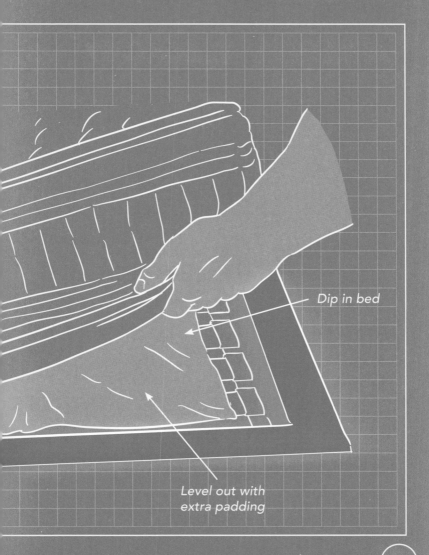

Dip in bed

Level out with
extra padding

BEDROOM BLACKOUT

Picture the scene: you're jet lagged and desperate for sleep as you enter your hotel room. You're all set to catch some serious Zs, but after drawing the curtains closed you find they don't meet in the middle properly, so there is an annoying beam of sleep-inhibiting light glaring in.

The answer is simple. Use a clothes hanger with clips (search the wardrobe for one, or ask at reception) to keep them firmly shut and relish that sweet, sweet sleep.

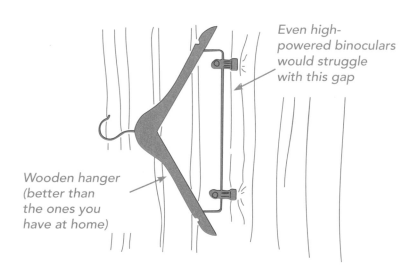

Even high-powered binoculars would struggle with this gap

Wooden hanger (better than the ones you have at home)

PEG STANDS

There are so many challenges to achieving a civilised holiday experience. If you've made the effort to keep your toothbrush nice and germ-free in transit, you don't want to mess it all up by resting it on a potentially unsanitary surface if there's no holder provided.

So be sure to pack a clothes peg in your washbag. Open it, grasp your toothbrush somewhere near the middle and prop it up away from the surface.

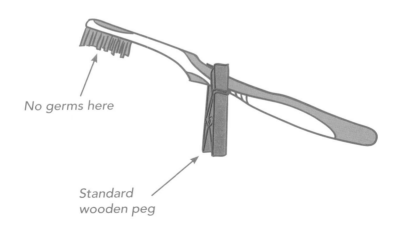

No germs here

Standard
wooden peg

BLACKOUT

Hotels are full of different people. Some of them will be pleasant, some of them will be downright annoying. And when those of the more bothersome persuasion can be heard being bothersome outside your door (which happens to not quite reach the floor, or perhaps has no draught excluder fitted) while you're sleeping, you're going to get angry.

But save yourself the spike in blood pressure and use this hack. Roll up a towel and push it under the door to muffle the sound and any light that also might be disturbing your blissful sleep.

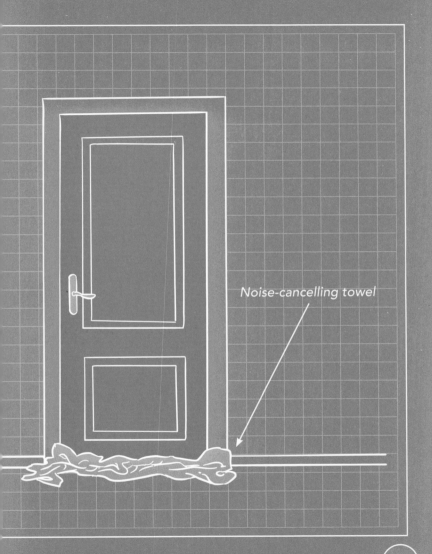

Noise-cancelling towel

89

HUNG OUT TO DRY

More upmarket and traditional hotels will have a laundry service to help if you need something washed and pressed, but if you're staying somewhere a little less fancy, you'll need another option.

If you're desperate to wash an item of clothing, head to the bathroom to see if it has a towel radiator. If so, give your garment a hand-wash (shampoo will work, if you can't get hold of actual detergent), wring out thoroughly and hang it up to dry on the radiator. You might have to do some work with the iron afterwards (fingers crossed you have one in your room!) but you can rest assured in smug satisfaction that you can enjoy freshly laundered undies for free.

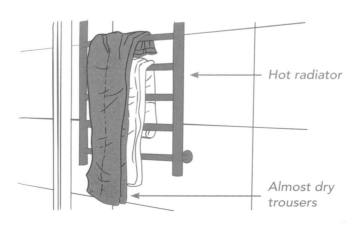

Hot radiator

Almost dry trousers

PRIVATE BUNK

Hostel accommodation isn't renowned for offering privacy – but you wouldn't have booked it if you weren't aware of this! However, while most fellow hostellers will be agreeable, there will be times you want to create a sense of your own space and this hack shows you how.

If you are able to nab the bottom bunk, ask reception for a spare sheet (or use a towel, if it's big enough) and throw them over the bunk's bars, thus creating for yourself a rather fetching privacy screen. Just go easy on the lights and sounds, or your roommates might think you're putting on some sort of low-budget shadow-puppet show.

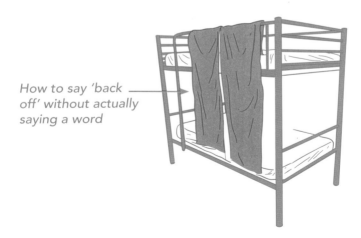

How to say 'back off' without actually saying a word

CLEAN-FREAK CUTLERY

Hostel hygiene can be another area of concern for the more germophobic of guests. This could apply to any establishment, of course, but as hostels are usually 'budget' in all areas you might be extra concerned about little things like cutlery.

If this is the case, you have two options. One, be sure to pack your own spork (a spoon and fork in one). Two, get yourself down to a local cafe (or a supermarket) and stock up on some disposable cutlery. And you might want to get some anti-bac spray while you're out, too.

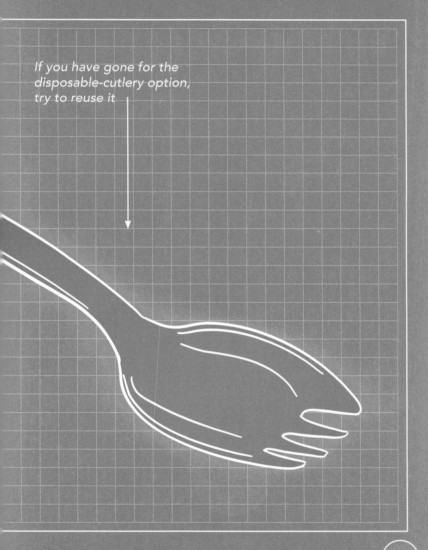

If you have gone for the disposable-cutlery option, try to reuse it

'DO NOT DISTURB'

If you're keeping valuables in the room you're staying in, it's always advisable to take reasonable precautions to protect your things. This might mean using a safe (if one is present) for your holiday money, or stashing your passport in a pair of pants (ones that look like they're 10 years old should do the trick!). But even with these measures in place, you can do a bit more.

Put your mind at ease and pop the 'do not disturb' sign on your door while out to deter well-meaning and not-so-well-meaning visitors alike.

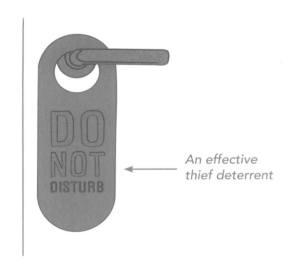

An effective thief deterrent

STAY SWITCHED ON

Big places like hotels use a lot of juice, so it's cool when they are energy-conscious and have one of those card devices to control the power in their rooms. But it's not so cool when you're melting in 40°C heat and you want to leave the air con on while you're out – or when you're intent on charging your phone for an all-important Facebook update.

To free yourself from the shackles of the card-in-the-slot system, try using an old credit card, membership card, or even a business card in your room key's place. Just remember to take it with you when you leave!

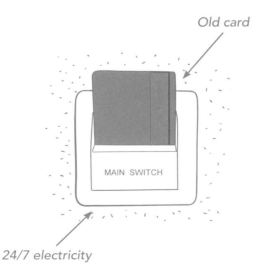

Old card

MAIN SWITCH

24/7 electricity

DIY COOLER

If you're staying in a hot country in a room with only a fan for air conditioning, you're in a real pickle. But don't wait around for the hotel or hostel to get their act together – hack your way to cool, cool victory.

Acquire a broad, shallow container – you might already have something like this in your room – perhaps the tray that the kettle is sitting on, but if not, see if you can get one from reception. It could be a drinks tray or a baking tray. Next, place it in front of your fan and fill it with iced water (not too close – remember water and electricity don't mix!). The fan will work to disperse moisture throughout the room, therefore cooling the temperature overall.

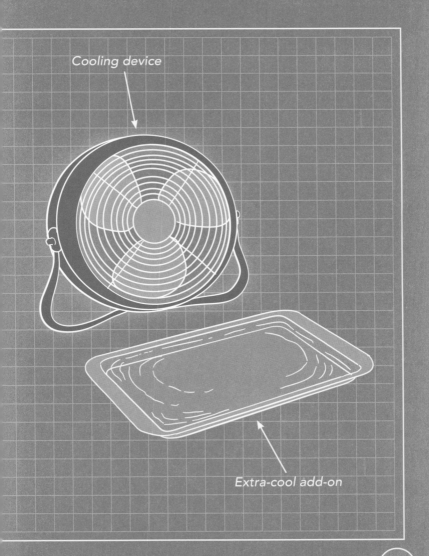

Cooling device

Extra-cool add-on

97

DORMITORY DINING

The average hotel room is kitted out for two things – washing and sleeping. You might also get a tiny table, with a kettle and fiddly sachets of coffee or tea, and a token chair, but if you want to eat anything substantial in your room, especially if you have kids, it's going to be awkward. Unless you use this hack.

Break out the ironing board, which is usually stashed somewhere in a wardrobe, and use it as an impromptu dining table. Set up the ironing board next to the bed so diners have somewhere to sit. This will significantly de-*crease* your chances of making a mess (see what I did there?).

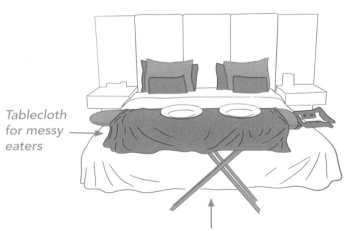

Tablecloth for messy eaters

Recreating a fine-dining experience

GRUB GRAB

This hack is for those who are not ashamed to scrimp. Eating lunch abroad is always tricky – chances are that on an average day you would just make something basic like a sandwich, but in a hotel this might not even be available, let alone affordable – and the same goes for eating out. In which case, you might want to make the most of the breakfast buffet.

But don't stuff yourself with an entire day's worth of food! Instead, make sure you fill up enough so you won't want lunch.

On your marks, get set, eat!

HIKING AND CAMPING HACKS

Travelling on foot is one of life's old-school pleasures. Yet, amazingly, before the horse and cart, the bicycle, trains, planes and Uber, people actually had to use their own two legs to get from one place to another. Yes, even if it was raining. But nowadays we do it for fun. And fun it is, if you're wise enough to hack your way to preparation. This chapter will show you how.

EMERGENCY CRAYONS

A steady source of light is key when you're hiking or camping. Away from your campfire, you might find you need to shed light on various activities and in the absence of a torch (or one that has a working battery!) you can use this hack.

Wax crayons with paper casing – good for colouring, great for burning in a candle-like fashion when there are no other light sources to hand. You can get up to half an hour from a lit crayon – just don't use your favourite colour, otherwise your artwork will suffer!

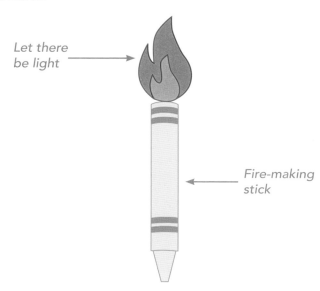

Let there be light

Fire-making stick

BLISTER RESISTER

There's nothing like a blister on your sole to slow your stride to an awkward hobble. And with blisters on both feet you might resemble somebody who has spent too long in the pub. But if you think ahead, you can avoid this.

If you're a regular walker, you should have an idea of where you might develop blisters. With this in mind, before you put your socks on, apply petroleum jelly to the parts of your feet prone to blisters. If you aren't a regular walker, then apply a light coating all over your feet, but especially the heel and sides. This will help to prevent rubbing and, hopefully, blisters!

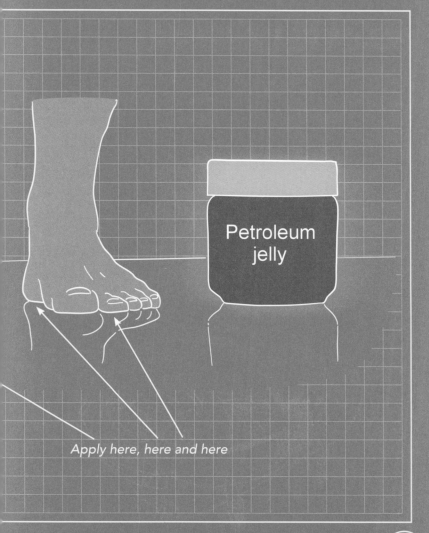

Petroleum jelly

Apply here, here and here

103

BACKPACK LINER

When you're out on a long walk, bad weather can be a real drag. Presuming you're hiking with a backpack, you should have had the sense to bring along, say, waterproof clothing for when it rains. But what about the bag itself?

It's no good trying to stay dry if your change of clothes is going to get wet. One way to help ensure this doesn't happen is by lining your backpack with a bin bag. If your backpack is waterproof already, a bin liner is a great way of keeping damp items away from dry ones, if your waterproof clothes aren't doing what they should!

Unreasonably heavy backpack

Super-cheap but effective bin liner

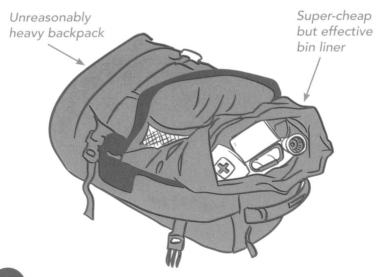

DIY FIRE STARTERS

If your hiking trip is going to feature a bit of wild camping (always read up on the camping laws of the country you are visiting before you go), you'll need to have a few basic survival skills. One of the most important is starting a fire. If you're in rugged country, this might be essential for survival; if you're at a campsite, this will be essential for toasting marshmallows. Either way, there's a hack to make it easier.

Coating cotton pads thoroughly in wax or covering cotton balls with petroleum jelly, making sure you leave a clean spot to hold on to, will create a flammable firestarter. Ignite the pad or ball, place it at the heart of your kindling and away you go.

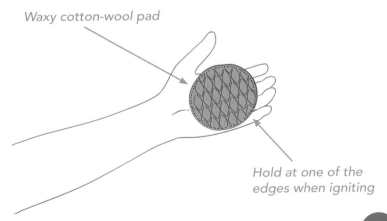

Waxy cotton-wool pad

Hold at one of the edges when igniting

WASH AND GO!

When you're camping or even on an extended walk, clothing issues are not something you need to be dealing with. Perhaps you've slipped and fallen in something brown and sticky (no, not a stick) and you're desperate to purge your garments – but you're miles away from a washing machine. Well, you can put a peg on your nose or you can use this hack.

Be sure to pack a large, durable ziplock bag. Stuff the soiled garment into the bag along with a small pinch or drop of laundry detergent, or some 'wash leaves' which you can buy from outdoor stores, and some water (hot or cold). You might have to beg for water at a local residence if you don't have any to spare from your bottle. Mix everything well using your hands for 5 minutes, before sealing and leaving to soak for 10 minutes. Then squeeze as much water out as possible before rinsing with clean water and squeezing again. Dry on an elastic travel washing line or hang it up. If using this hack while hiking or outdoors, make sure to use 100% biodegradable soap.

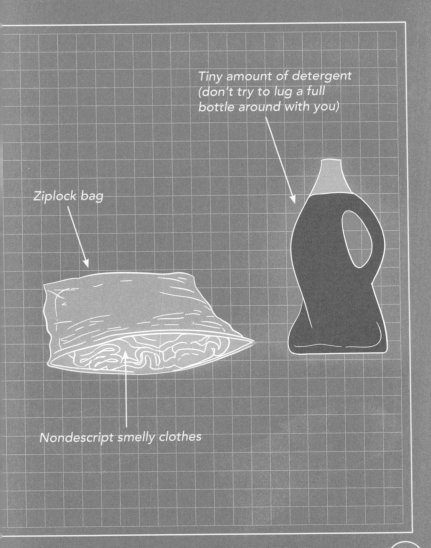

Tiny amount of detergent (don't try to lug a full bottle around with you)

Ziplock bag

Nondescript smelly clothes

SUPERCHARGED SLEEPING BAG

If a cold night is on the cards, your sleeping bag needs to be up to the job. If you're concerned it might not be (or perhaps you can't afford the extortionate price for a new one) consider this hack to boost your night-time comfort.

Those heat reflectors that sensible people put in their car windows to reflect the sun are naturally good at reflecting heat. So by slipping one (or two) into your sleeping bag, you'll create a layer of heat-reflecting insulation. You'll be as toasty as a turkey in tinfoil on gas mark 4.

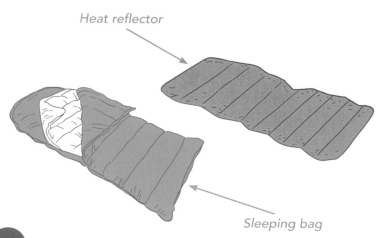

Heat reflector

Sleeping bag

MOSQUITO MANAGEMENT

At the end of a long day of walking, you'll want to rest easy. Depending on where in the world you are, you will have to consider different possibilities for animal annoyances. One that's pretty universal is mosquitoes. These high-pitched buzzing biting machines can ruin your night. Here's a simple hack to help.

When pitching your tent, position the opening so it's facing into the wind. That way, the menacing mozzies will be deterred from entering your tent, leaving you to dream peacefully about lollipops and unicorns.

Incoming wind

No mosquitoes in sight

KEY FLOAT

The wilderness is great for getting away from it all. The only problem is, you have to get back to it all, and usually this will involve car and house keys. The last thing you want is for either of these to go missing in the woods – or even worse at the bottom of a lake or river! This hack will show you how to avoid these horrible eventualities.

Take your key (or bunch of keys – but not too many) and attach it to a wine cork. To do this, take an eyelet screw and drive it into the top of the cork, then simply attach it to your key ring. What you're left with is an infinitely more spottable and less sinkable key. (Note, this won't work for keyless fobs – water and electrical components will never get along!)

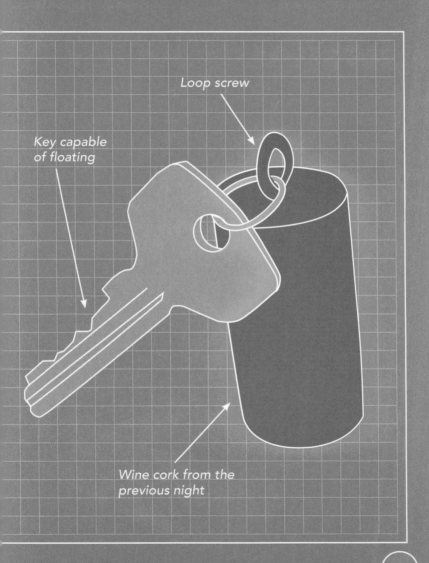

Loop screw

Key capable
of floating

Wine cork from the
previous night

111

SUPPLY SEND-OUT

Here's one for when you're on a serious trek, where overloading your backpack would be a major drawback. If you're on a multi-day hike and you need to travel lighter than you'd like to, all is not lost. Like the explorers in those old movies that your grandad loves to watch, you can set yourself up to receive much-needed supply boxes in designated places.

This sounds pretty dramatic, but in reality it's as simple as packing up weighty essentials and sending them to a post-office collection point that's en route. The main bonus is that you can travel light while still acquiring your supplies – even if those supplies consist of copious amounts of sweets and cans of beer!

Full of essentials that are less essential than the essentials back home you realise you should have sent

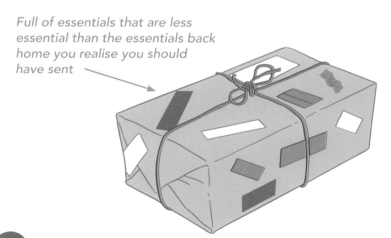

BOTTLE BOOST

Hydration is key when you're hiking. Investing in a sturdy metal water bottle is a great idea – as opposed to a plastic bottle, a metal one will hold the temperature of the liquid placed inside it for longer. However, you can give it a boost and make it even better with this hack.

Wrapping your bottle in duct tape will increase its temperature-holding potential. In cold weather, it will also protect your fingers from a chill when holding the bottle. So it's a win-win!

Fancy metal water bottle

Insulating tape

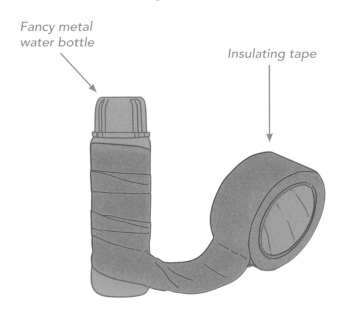

SUSPEND-A-SNACK

When camping, the last thing you want is to wake up to find a horse's head in your tent. Attached to a horse's body, of course, and rooting around in your bag of food. This goes double for rats, bears and overly friendly locals.

To avoid unwanted attention from local wildlife, including insects, hang your food supplies up on the branch of a tree. (Alternatively, a bear canister, which is essentially a reinforced can that seals in scents and is tough enough to withstand an assault by a ravenous mammal, can be used). Just remember that wherever your food stash ends up, you're going to have to be able to retrieve it!

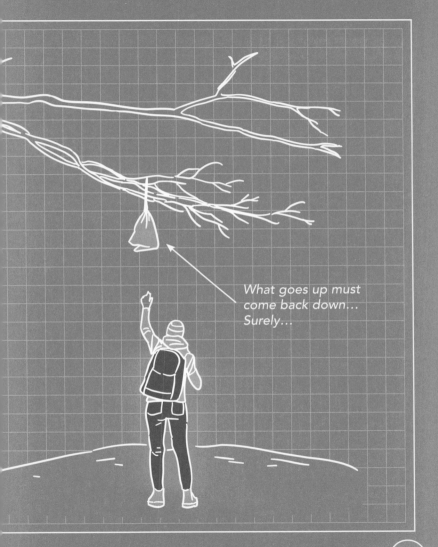

What goes up must come back down... Surely...

TAPE TRAIL

Even seasoned trekkers lose their way from time to time. If your travels have taken you into dense forest or woodland, relocating your campsite can prove tricky, especially at night. You can take the stress out of the situation with this simple hack.

Invest in some brightly coloured biodegradable tape, which you can use to mark out a key route through difficult environs. Leave small tabs in easy-to-spot places, or if you're really in the thick of it, and you're not going very far, run a longer stretch of tape out at waist height.

It marks the spot!

HANG 'N' HIKE

If you're unfortunate enough to have got caught in the rain during your travels, you'll need to dry your clothes out asap. But what if you're on a schedule and you don't have time to wait for them to dry? Or you want to take advantage of the sun that has suddenly decided to show up after you set off for your day of hiking?

Pack some carabiners in your bag for this hack. If you're in too much of a rush to wait for your clothes to dry, why not pin them to your backpack and let them air out as you walk? If that elusive sun is shining, they'll be dry in no time!

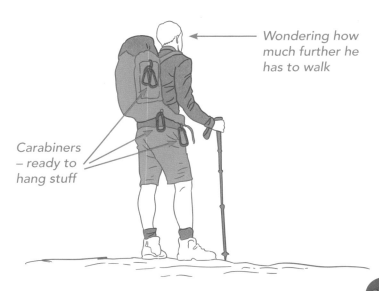

Wondering how much further he has to walk

Carabiners – ready to hang stuff

GET BUSY WITH BEESWAX

If you're keen on the environment as well as staying dry while out walking, this one is for you. Waterproofing your gear is an essential precaution for any trek – however, most spray-on proofers are made up of various synthetic chemicals. If you're keen on avoiding these, here's a natural alternative.

Beeswax is featured in many proofing products anyway, but used in its pure form, it's doing a similar job without having been heavily processed. It can be rubbed directly on to garments, bags and shoes – just expect them to be a little waxy and pleasantly fragrant as a result.

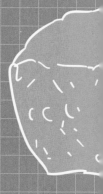

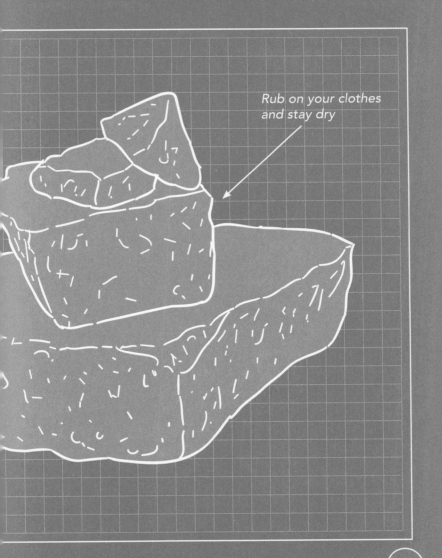

Rub on your clothes and stay dry

DRY BOOTS

Whether your boots are wet from working up a sweat or from trudging through huge puddles or a rainstorm, as soon as you have the chance you'll want to let them dry. Here's a hack to help you do just that.

Ball up some newspaper and stuff it (not too tightly!) into each of your boots. The paper will absorb the moisture and help dry your boots out much quicker than heat alone. If you've finished walking for the day, replace the paper after a couple of hours.

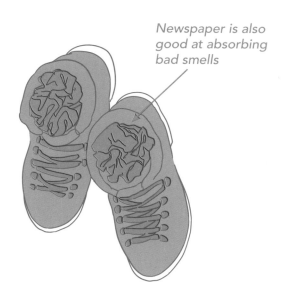

Newspaper is also good at absorbing bad smells

LIQUID LANTERN

Camping brings many challenges, one of which is seeing when it's dark. There are no light switches in a tent (at least not the ones I stay in), so you'll need a light source of your own. If you're travelling light on a hike, you don't want a bulky lantern, just a head torch. But with this hack you can have both.

Take a see-through bottle, the bigger the better, and fill it with water. Take your head torch and strap it to the outside of the bottle so the beam is directed inside. Turn it on and, hey presto, you have a dazzling lantern, as the light from the torch is refracted by the water in the bottle.

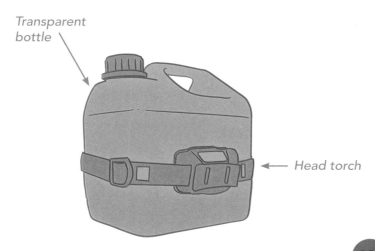

Transparent bottle

Head torch

DRINKS CAN CAMPING STOVE

This hack involves quite a bit of work and requires patience and care to avoid sharp edges. However, if you're in need of a controlled source of heat for your camping shenanigans, it's worth it.

You'll need the bottoms of two drinks cans, cut away from the rest of the can (use scissors), each with about an inch of can left. In one of the bottoms, pierce a series of holes around the rim (use the point of the scissors or a sharp knife) and a slightly larger one in the centre of the concave bottom. Next, slot your two bottoms together, with the pierced one on top, and add some flammable liquid (alcohol solution) into the top hole. When ignited, you will effectively have a mini-gas ring, with flames emerging from the pierced ring of holes! Useful for heating small amounts of water, to purify or for tea, in the absence of firewood.

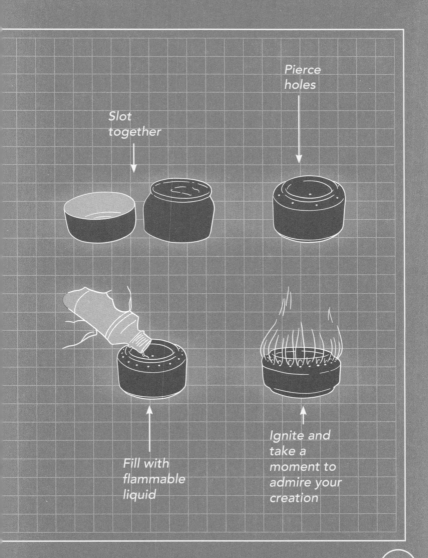

Slot together

Pierce holes

Fill with flammable liquid

Ignite and take a moment to admire your creation

ON A ROLL

Everybody poops. And of course it's true, even hikers and campers need to answer the call of nature. But, again, you don't want to be weighing your pack down by filling it with bulky items. So, is there such a thing as a non-bulky toilet roll? You bet!

Simply remove the cardboard tube and squash the paper roll down as flat as it can go. You now have a much more compact toilet roll, and you can do your business without inconvenience.

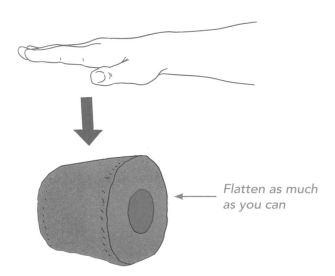

Flatten as much as you can

LOG JAM

While on a trek you might well encounter parts of a route where you need to traverse water. It might be that some kind fellow has created a crossing over a stream using a sturdy log (sometimes good folk lay down thick logs in areas that are especially prone to getting boggy too), but if you're a little unsteady on your feet, especially when you're carrying a heavy backpack, it's best to have a few tricks up your sleeve to prevent a slip.

One of these tricks is to sprinkle a handful of silt or fine grit over the log before you set foot on it. Salt will work, too, if you have any. This will improve your grip and help you avoid taking an early mud bath.

If you fall in, see hack 'Hung Out to Dry', page 90

Salt/grit

BEACH HACKS

Who doesn't enjoy a relaxing stroll on the beach? People who are allergic to sand, for one. But for the rest of us, it's a place where we can recharge and revitalise with an intake of salty air and warm sunshine. But even with this simple pleasure, there are hacks to be noted. This chapter will show you how to have fun in the sun without getting sand in places you'd prefer it not to be.

WRAP IT UP!

Sun, sea and sand are all well and good for enjoyment, but they don't mix so well with electronics. You're bound to want to take various selfies while at the beach and send them to work colleagues to make them even more miserable than they already are, so use this hack to ensure your phone isn't messed up in the process.

Simply wrap your phone in a layer of cling film – it will then be protected from sand, spray and anything else that might negatively affect its performance, with the added bonus that the touchscreen should still work as normal.

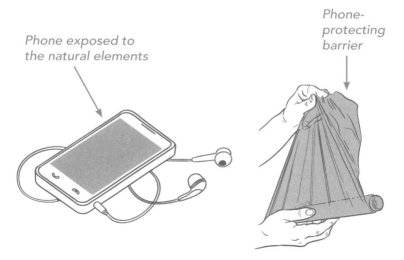

Phone exposed to the natural elements

Phone-protecting barrier

SAND-FREE SET-UP

A day at the beach can quickly turn into an annoyance if tiny bits of sand have managed to work their way into places they are not wanted – we're talking towels, food, drinks, bodily orifices. But there's a hack to help avoid this.

Set yourself up with a sand-free zone by bringing an old fitted bed sheet along to the party (don't use one from the hotel! This is more of a staycation hack). If you lay it down and place heavy items like bags and coolers in each of the corners, then turn the sheet up so it hugs them, you'll have created a little haven against sand blowing up on to your lunch, etc. and a space where you can sit that isn't sandy – just don't walk any sand in yourself, or it'll end up as a sandpit!

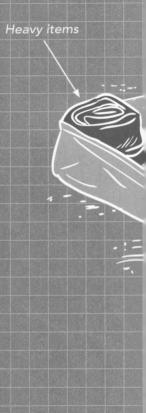

Heavy items

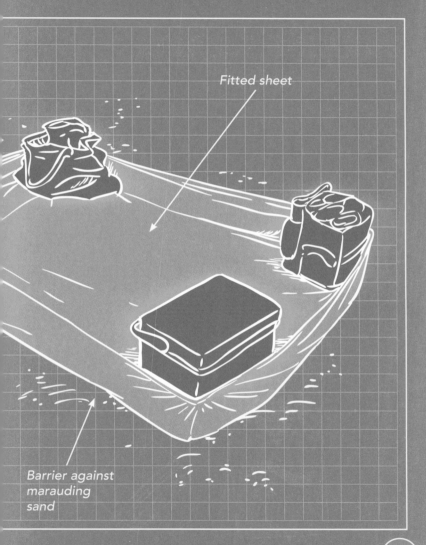

Fitted sheet

Barrier against
marauding
sand

129

TANNING SECRETS

Imagine the scene. It's a lovely day and you fancy lying out in the sun, generally cooking for a few hours. But what do you do with your valuables? Your bag is an obvious target for thieves and chances are your swimming costume doesn't have pockets!

So use an empty sun lotion bottle instead. Simply clean it out and, presuming the top of the bottle is wide enough, slot your valuables inside. If you want to hide larger items, like a phone, carefully cut the top part of the bottle off at a wide point, insert your bits and pieces, and then push the top part back into the bottle, beyond where you made your cut.

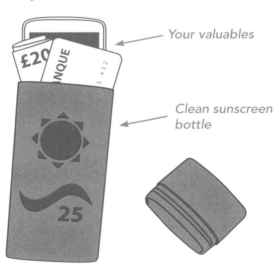

Your valuables

Clean sunscreen bottle

BABY POWDER BRUSH-OFF

If you haven't managed to avoid getting various parts of your body caked in sand (and, let's face it, if you have you're some kind of miracle worker) and there are no showers readily available, you'll need a way to de-sand yourself before even thinking about getting dressed, getting in a car, or returning to your room.

Avoid getting sand in literally everything you come into contact with by using this hack to remove it. Grab some baby powder and shake some on to the sand-affected areas. Then simply brush it off and watch those pesky particles fall away.

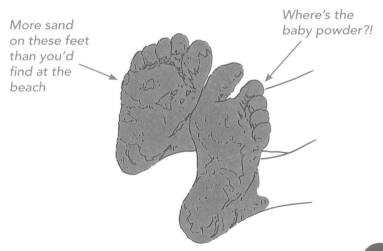

More sand on these feet than you'd find at the beach

Where's the baby powder?!

TOWEL POCKETS

Organising your essentials at the beach can be a pain, especially if you're prone to misplacing things five seconds after you handle them. Here's a clever way of keeping your belongings where you want them.

Add some pockets to your beach towel. It's a simple case of sacrificing an old towel (preferably one with complementary colours) and cutting it into squares large, or small, enough to make your pockets. Simply sew the squares on to your towel, remembering to leave one side unsewn for the opening, and you have a funky and functional beach towel.

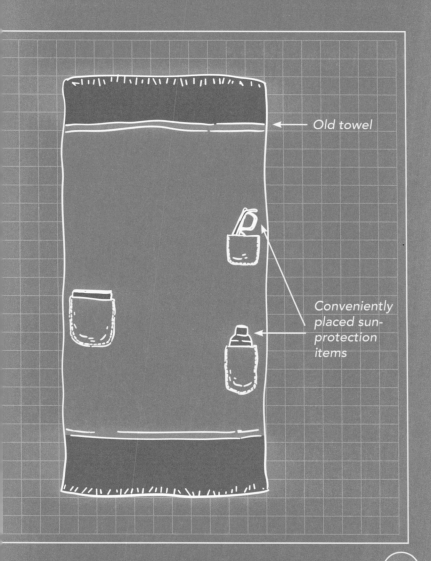

Old towel

Conveniently placed sun-protection items

ALOE CUBES

With all of the health warnings about excess exposure to UV rays, you really have no excuse for getting sunburn. But if you're out on a day trip enjoying yourself, you might forget to be vigilant with the sun cream. So what do you do when you've gone full lobster?

Start by squeezing out some aloe vera gel (not lotion) into an ice-cube tray. Let it freeze for 30 minutes to an hour and you have yourself a cool, soothing application that will help heal your skin and hide your shame.

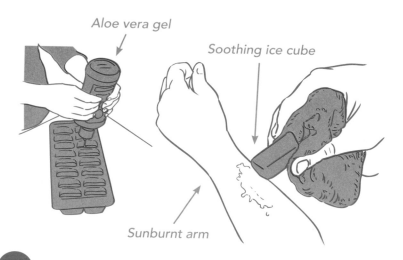

Aloe vera gel

Soothing ice cube

Sunburnt arm

CAR KEY COPY

Here's one for those of you who are wary of your car keys being ruined when you run like an excited child into the sea without thinking about the fact you have your keys on you.

Before your trip, pay a visit to a key-cutter and get a copy made of your ignition key. The key-cutter might helpfully inform you that the key will not start the car (it has to be from a dealer for this to be the case), but that's OK – you just want to get back into your car. When you arrive at the beach, lock your actual key in a safe place inside the car, taking the copy with you. You can now frolic in the sea as much as you like, since the copy is just a hunk of metal and not a sophisticated, electronic-filled genuine article.

Electronic-filled genuine article

Hunk of metal

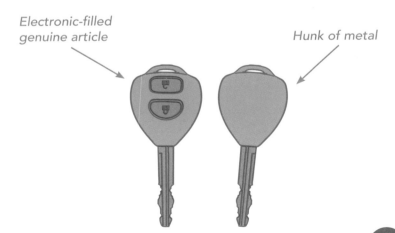

BUDGET BEACH FIRE

If you're planning on spending the night at the local beach - maybe you've got enough friends to have a party or, like me, you just like sitting by yourself staring at the flames - you might want to get a fire going. The first thing you should do is check to be sure this is allowed, but once you have the OK you can take advantage of this hack.

There are various ways to use household items to help you start your fire without the need to pay for firelighters. Lint from a tumble dryer stuffed into the spaces in an egg carton is a windproof way of getting your fire off to a good start. Smokin'.

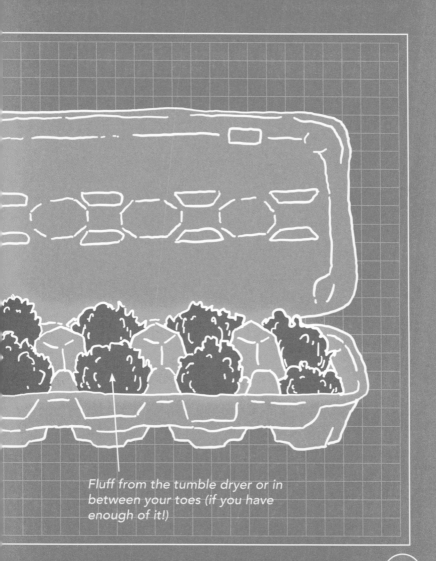

Fluff from the tumble dryer or in between your toes (if you have enough of it!)

WATER IN YOUR EARS

We've all been there. Whether at the pool or in the sea, if you dip your head under the water there's a good chance you'll be taking some of the water with you as it gets lodged in your ear canal. This is a definite no-go, especially when you're on holiday – how will you hear the wonderful cabaret singer that's on at your hotel later? Here's how.

Take a deflated balloon with you if you think you'll be going for a swim. If your ears are feeling clogged after you've been for a dip, just blow the balloon up and your ears should pop a treat.

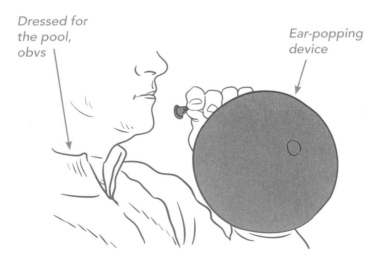

Dressed for the pool, obvs

Ear-popping device

COOL-GRIP STEERING WHEEL

There's probably some science behind it, but somehow things left out in the sun can get skin-searingly hot. Ever tried walking on hot sand without footwear – it hurts like hell. And it's not just sand – it can affect your car too. So if you decide to drive to the beach, here's a helpful tip.

If you're not lucky enough to have a sun deflector for your windscreen, you can at least keep your steering wheel from reaching burning point by rotating it 180 degrees once you've parked. That way, the sun will be scorching what is technically the bottom of the steering wheel, leaving the top, upon your return, unscathed.

Just remember to turn it back to its normal position when you drive off

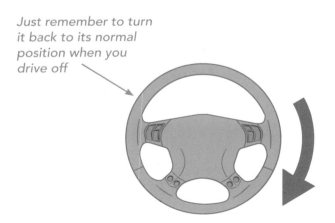

DELUXE BEACH TOWEL EXPERIENCE

So you've managed to score an extra-soft dinosaur beach towel – it can't get any better, right? Wrong! You can be even more comfortable and look even more cool.

This one requires quite a bit of home prep, but it's totally worth it. You'll need a bed pillow you're willing to dedicate to the cause and another beach towel on top of the one you have. The first step is to sew the bottom of the second towel to the top of your first towel. Next, place your pillow at the head of the first towel/bottom of the second, and fold the second towel over to encase it. Sew around the pillow and trim off any excess towel, so you have a neat towel-based pillowcase. What you're left with is a ridiculously comfortable beach towel.

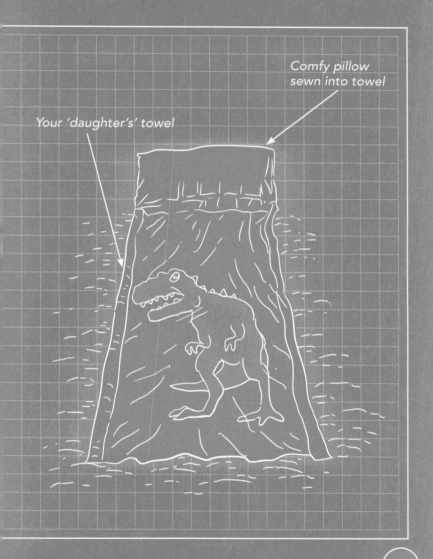

Comfy pillow
sewn into towel

Your 'daughter's' towel

141

BITING-BUG BANISHER

Biting bugs can even attack at the beach. Unbelievably, nature thinks beaches are also environments for animals and not just places for holidaymakers to enjoy. I know! So what are you to do when you're out on a romantic evening stroll and the bugs decide they want in on some of the action and start biting?

Mosquitoes in particular can be repelled by creamy baby oil. It's bound to be cheaper than actual mozzie spray, and it has the added bonus of being a moisturiser!

Mosquitoes on a mission ——→

←—— *Not for long*

FLIP-FLOP FIX

What do you do when your favourite flip-flops have bitten the dust and the thong has broken? Hack it!

Start by cutting the now-flailing thong completely off where it joins the main strap. Next, grab a hair tie and fold it around the centre of the strap. Take one of the loops and thread it through the other and tighten, so you're left with just one loop. Thread this loop through the hole in the flip-flop. Then, finish by tying a knot in the loop, big enough so it won't pull back through. Boom! Your flip-flops are back in the game.

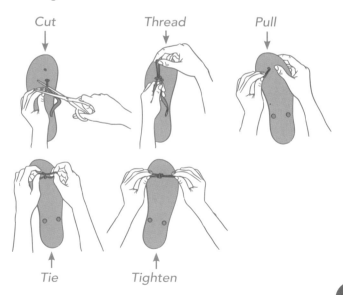

BEACH BLANKET

Beach towels, as you might expect, are made for the beach. But they're still essentially towels, which means that, once wet, they are sand magnets. If this is going to be an issue for you, there is another way to set up camp on the beach.

Opt for a waterproof picnic blanket instead. Like the name says, it's waterproof, so it won't get damp and collect sand, yet it will still provide a comfortable base for you to enjoy the beach experience.

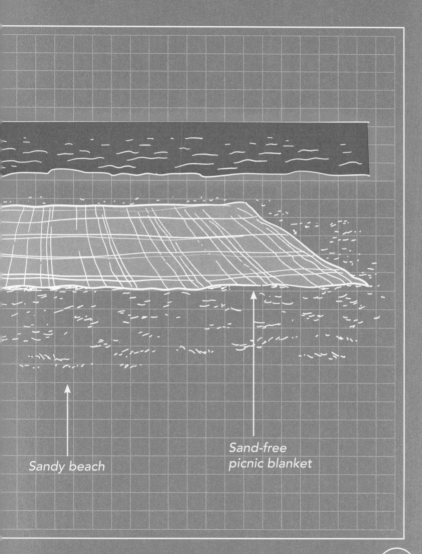

Sandy beach

Sand-free
picnic blanket

145

CITY HACKS

Some people (strange though they may be, in my opinion) prefer to escape to a bustling metropolis when on vacation. Cities offer a cornucopia of exciting experiences, but they also pose their own unique challenges. Travelling around without getting lost or ripped off are two of them, as well as negotiating the eternally confusing matter of how much to tip for a meal. Worry not – it's all explained in this chapter.

OFFLINE MAPS

Everybody with a smartphone is used to using a map to navigate. For getting around in cities, it's a revelation. But, of course, most will rely on a consistent internet connection, which can be costly if you are abroad. The best way to overcome this is by downloading a map app that works offline.

And there are now plenty to choose from. Many of them have the same functions as your favourite online map app – they will point out bars, restaurants and other points of interest, and will allow you to 'pin' desired destinations for easy navigation. All without a Wi-Fi hotspot in sight!

Surely you don't need a map to get there?! ⟶

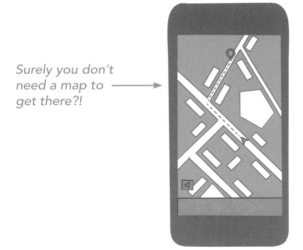

BE SCAM SAFE

It's pretty common now for taxis to be fitted with card machines for fares, but for some less-than-honest drivers, this is just an excuse to cheat their customers out of money. When you've reached your destination, some drivers will claim that the card machine is out of service or that it's tied up downloading software, meaning you have to reach for your cash. After you've done so, the devious driver will then claim he has no change, so you'll end up paying more than you should.

The best way to avoid this is to pre-book your ride and pay over the phone. Either that, or be sure to be at your most stubborn and insist that you will wait for the machine to finish its update before you pay.

Mercenary taxi driver

Scam-free system

149

CITY AIRPORT PICKUPS

If you're flying into a city, chances are it's going to be pretty busy. The busier it is, the more competition there will be between taxi companies to land those juicy tourist fares, so airports tend to select 'approved' companies. And of course this means they can charge what they like, since you have a limited choice.

Avoid this by first taking a (usually free) shuttle bus to an area outside of the airport. From this point, you will be free to use a potentially much cheaper taxi service (just make sure you have a few numbers to try!).

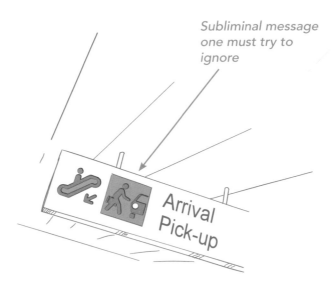

Subliminal message one must try to ignore

Arrival Pick-up

CASH STASH

Bumbags (or fanny packs, if you're American) are not just a tragic fashion item for those who grew up in the 1980s and early 1990s. If you're in a city, it's a sad fact that you're generally more likely to be a victim of pickpockets – more people often means more problems. So what can you do to keep your cash and other valuables safe?

You guessed it. Strap on that bumbag and pretend that you're back in the age of leg warmers and Hypercolor T-shirts. Works even better for those of a hipster persuasion, since you'll be wearing it 'ironically'. The reality is, you'll have a small, concealed place for your stuff.

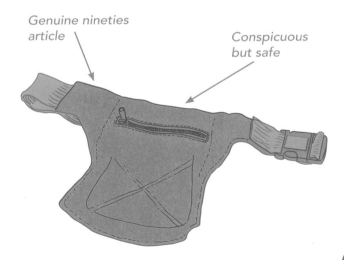

Genuine nineties article

Conspicuous but safe

PICNIC PERKS

Lunch in the city feels so cosmopolitan, but chances are you'll want to avoid paying swanky city eatery prices, so let go of the fantasy and use this hack instead.

If you want a city lunch, simply visit a local supermarket or deli and take advantage of a public outdoor space with a picnic instead. Admittedly, this will be weather permitting, but it will also give you the chance to experience some local flavours (gastronomic and cultural) and it won't break the bank. You might even meet a few friendly dogs, and who doesn't want that? (Just as long as they're not helping themselves to your club sandwich.)

So sophisticated!

153

TIP SMART

When you're abroad and dining out, it's easy to get wrapped up in the awesome experience of it all. It's new and exciting, and if you have a good meal on top of that, you might want to show your gratitude by leaving a nice tip. But think twice before you do.

There's absolutely nothing wrong with tipping – and in most cases it should be encouraged – but check your bill to see if service charge has already been added. If, as in many tourist-heavy places, it has been, there's no need for you to feel obliged to tip – you're already covered and you can leave knowing the staff will not curse you under their breath. If you do want to tip, try to find out what the standard is for the country you're visiting.

Generous tip IMO

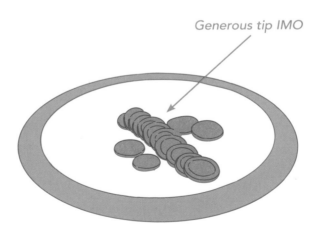

GO LOCAL

It's the traveller's eternal dilemma – you want to see the sights, because they're popular for a reason, but this means falling into a tourist trap and prices are likely to be high. But if you resist the pull of the touristy approach, you can reap the rewards.

For instance, the best way to get a less tourist-centric experience of any new city is to avoid getting a taxi and travel by public transport. It's cheaper for one, and you'll be treated to an experience of the lesser-known areas – some might be unremarkable, but others could be hidden gems, far from the tourist crowd.

See new stuff

Take the tram

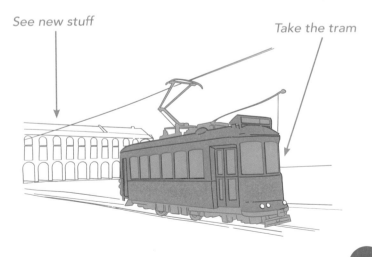

FREE FUN!

When you're in a city full of famous tourist attractions, you might be forgiven for thinking that you're in for a costly time. But often you'd be wrong.

It's worth doing your research before heading out to that museum, art gallery or famous building on your must-see list, since you might well find that discounts are readily available. For example, many places offer reduced prices for students and those over 65. You might also be able to attend for free at an 'off-peak' time or on certain days.

Bargains, bargains, bargains

SURVIVAL HACKS

If your idea of travel involves adventure – that is, journeying to remote or even potentially dangerous locations – then you're braver than I am! But for many people this is exactly what travelling means – taking calculated risks in challenging environments to experience a once-in-a-lifetime thrill. This chapter will cover you for everything from finding your way in the dark to ensuring you have clean water to drink, making your adventure more bearable if things do go south.

HYGIENIC HYDRATION

Clean water is essential to life in any situation. So if you're in a remote location and find yourself without it, it can spell trouble. Presuming you can source water, here's how to ensure it's drinkable.

The easiest way is to always carry water-purifying tablets. Adding these to your H_2O will ensure it's safe. You can even stock up on water-purifying straws, which have the same effect. Boiling your water, or using a water-purifying bottle, are other ways to ensure your thirst is quenched safely.

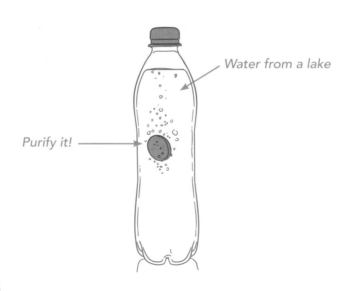

Water from a lake

Purify it!

DAYLIGHT MEASURE

Imagine you're out walking – it's getting late and you're worried that you might not make it back to camp before dark. Put your mind at ease (or not) by estimating the amount of daylight left using nothing other than your bare hand.

Hold your arm parallel to the horizon with your fingers straight and your thumb tucked in. Line your index finger with the bottom of the sun and count how many finger widths there are between the sun and the horizon. Each finger equals roughly 15 minutes of daylight. If there are five minutes of daylight left, start running!

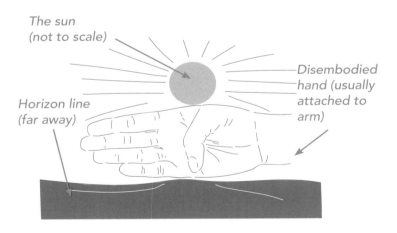

The sun
(not to scale)

Disembodied
hand (usually
attached to
arm)

Horizon line
(far away)

FINDING NORTH AT NIGHT

If you're out in the wild and you need to find your way without a compass, there's a simple solution. (But let's just take a minute here to say that you should NEVER embark on an unguided trip without a map and a compass!)

Presuming you don't have any options left, you can navigate by finding the North Star (Polaris), as long as you're in the northern hemisphere. First you need to locate the Plough, aka the Big Dipper. This is possibly the most well-known constellation, so if you don't know it, you should definitely learn it. At the end of the Plough that is furthest from its 'handle' you should be able to pick out the top-most star (on the top 'lip' of the Plough). From this point, extend your gaze in a straight line (away from the bottom of the Plough) until you see a distinctly bright star. This is Polaris, your north point.

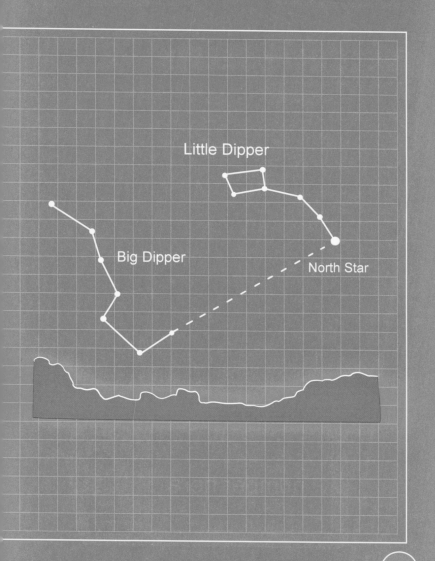

Little Dipper

Big Dipper

North Star

SECURITY SELFIE

Many people love to document their trips by taking countless photos – and why not? With digital cameras you can snap away almost without care. But if you lose your camera, this hack will provide you with the best chance of reclaiming it.

Before you set out on a snapping expedition, take a photo of a piece of paper with your name and contact number on it. That way, if your lost property is recovered, the finder will be able to contact its owner (you!).

If cameras are a thing of the past to you, try this hack with your smartphone

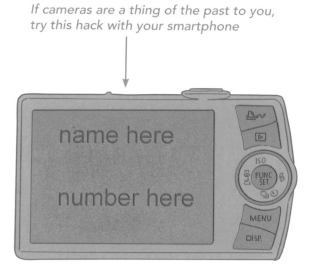

BEE- AND WASP-STING TREATMENT

Bees and wasps are commonly found almost everywhere around the world, and if you're unlucky enough to get stung by one you'll want to minimise the pain and annoyance by treating the sting. But what if you don't have your antihistamine? Here's what to do.

For acidic bee stings, make a paste out of baking powder and a small amount of water combined. For alkaline wasp stings, apply a mixture of one part vinegar and one part water. So instead of wasting money on antihistamines and sting cream, remember to pack a small amount of vinegar and baking powder if you're on an outdoor adventure!

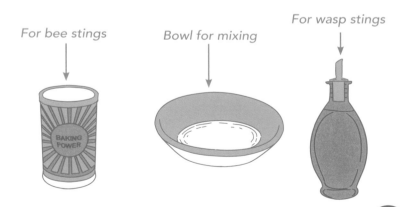

For bee stings

Bowl for mixing

For wasp stings

MOSQUITO BITE TREATMENT

Another winged menace that can add stress to an already stressful situation is the mosquito. Yes, by biting you they're just doing what comes naturally, but from your perspective you're left with at best an annoying lump, which if scratched can become infected. Resist the temptation with this hack.

Apply toothpaste to your bite as soon as you can. The mint will ease the itching and help you to get on with more important things.

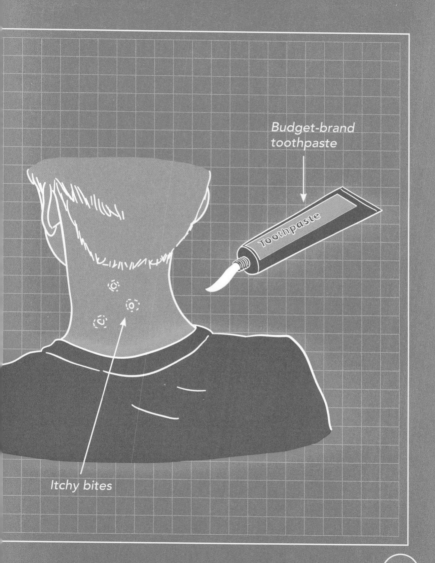

Budget-brand
toothpaste

Toothpaste

Itchy bites

TICK REMOVAL

Completing the trio of common insect terrors we have ticks. These tiny little bloodsuckers enjoy nothing more than burrowing into your skin for a delicious, bloody feast. Gross. They can also transmit diseases and again cause infections if the bites are scratched. A tick key is the easiest way to remove any unwanted hitchhikers, but if you don't have one here's what to do.

Break out the tweezers. Grasp the tick with the tweezers as close to the surface of the skin as you can and pull upward with a steady, even pressure. Carefully remove any parts that may linger in the skin before lightly washing the area with water. Dispose of the tick down the toilet, place in a sealed bag or wrap it securely in tape.

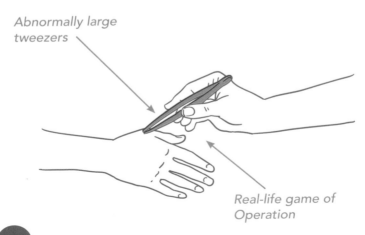

Abnormally large tweezers

Real-life game of Operation

TINY FIRST-AID KIT

It goes without saying that you should have a first-aid kit in your car, but what if you're travelling by a different mode of transport, or it's a hire car? Failing to prepare is preparing to fail, so be smart and create your own tiny medi-kit.

Take an old pill bottle (or an old film-roll holder if you can locate one) and fill it with essentials like plasters, small sections of bandage, safety pins and antiseptic cream. This will easily fit in the pocket of your jacket or your bag, ensuring you're covered for any minor scrapes.

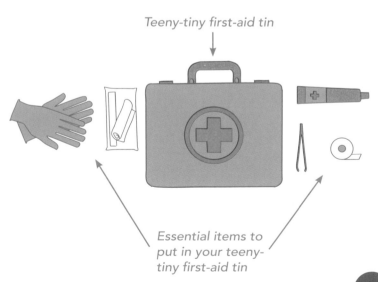

Teeny-tiny first-aid tin

Essential items to put in your teeny-tiny first-aid tin

167

BATTERY BURNER

Here's a way of making trash into something that will help you live a little longer. For this hack you'll need a chewing-gum wrapper – the shiny metallic kind – and an AA battery. Both of these items are easy to bring along on any outdoor trip and this hack shows you how they can make fire.

It's really quite simple: tear off two thin strips of the shiny wrapper, place one at each end of the battery, shiny side down, and bend the free ends over, so they are not near your fingers. Within a short time you will see the free ends of the wrappers burst into flame.

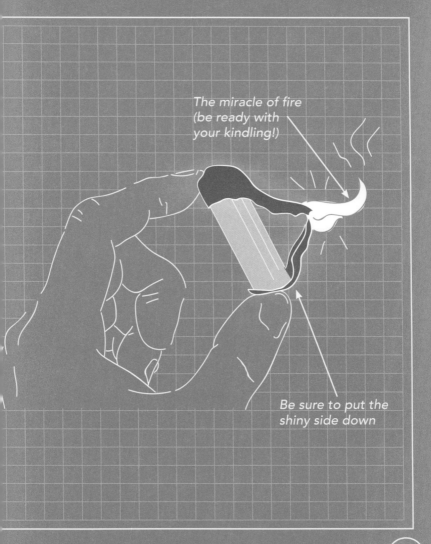

The miracle of fire
(be ready with
your kindling!)

Be sure to put the
shiny side down

EVERYTHING ELSE

Some hacks defy categorisation. You'll find all of the following useful, but you might not have so many occasions to use them on your travels or they might just be a bit 'out there'. But you never know when you'll need that hack for beating blisters, or that secret method of counteracting turbulence by getting your groove on. Intrigued? Then read on!

SHAKE SAFE

If you're a fan of games that don't involve screens and in-app purchases – and perhaps do involve dice – you'll appreciate this hack. (Even better if you can get your kids, if you have them, to join in and play along with some old-fashioned fun!)

This can help wherever you find yourself, be it in a caravan in Skegness or a beach hut in Barbados. To ensure you don't lose them while playing, place your dice in a small plastic container. You can then shake and shimmy your dice to your heart's content, safe in the knowledge that they won't be going anywhere.

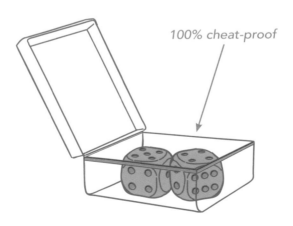

100% cheat-proof

GET JIGGY WITH THE TURBULENCE

This hack will work best if you have an embarrassment factor of zero, but it will pay off if you're someone who freaks out when you experience turbulence on the plane.

If the plane starts shaking, start dancing along with it. By gently jiggling yourself in your seat, you will counteract the aircraft's movement, meaning you don't feel the turbulence as much.

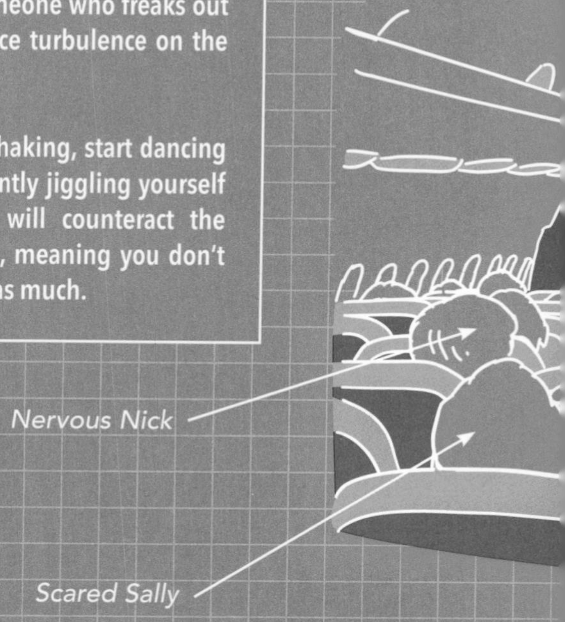

Nervous Nick

Scared Sally

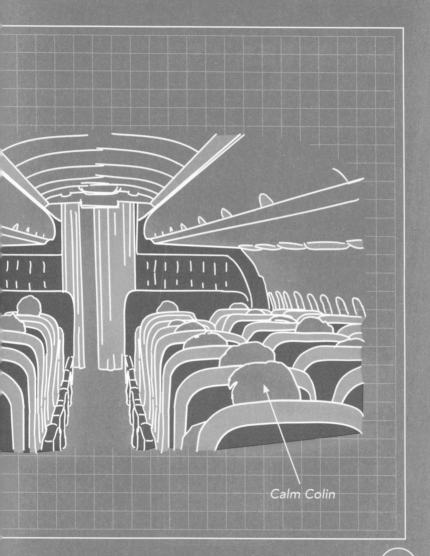

Calm Colin

173

GET ORGANISED

Some people find going on holiday a major stress. But for those of you who are willing to give it a go, you can get some help in the form of apps.

One to try is 'TripIt', where you send all email confirmations across and it can sort them out into a neat itinerary. Or there is 'Remember the Milk', which can help with organising lists for your holiday.

Smartphone required

POWDER YOUR 'DO

Summer sun is great, until the sweat and the oily hair kicks in. If you're a fellow sufferer, here's a neat trick to tame it.

Talcum powder can be used as a replacement for dry shampoo. It can also be used as a setting powder, to stop the sweat from allowing make-up to slide off your face. So you can stay looking fabulous even in the blistering heat.

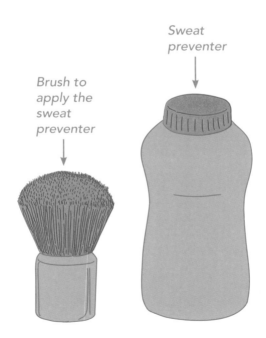

Sweat preventer

Brush to apply the sweat preventer

COMFY SANDALS

In hot weather you'll want to break out the sandals. I personally love a sock-and-sandal combo, but for those with more sophisticated tastes, you'll want to go sock-free. But if you do, and your sandals are new, you could run the risk of getting a blister or two.

To keep the pesky pain away, simply spray your ankles and toes with deodorant. The deodorant reduces moisture and friction, and thus decreases the chance of rubbing and blisters.

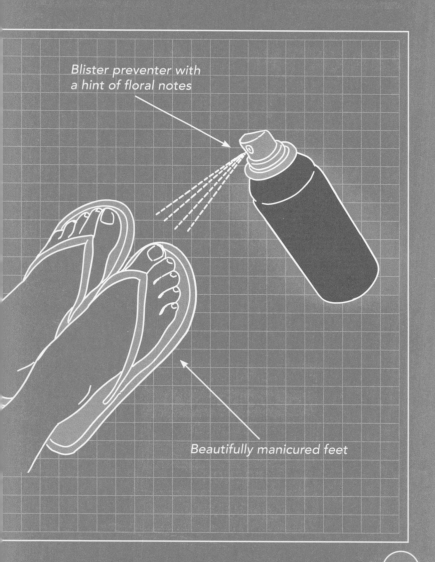

Blister preventer with a hint of floral notes

Beautifully manicured feet

177

LEARN THE LINGO

One of the most unfortunate habits of international travellers is the tendency to presume your native tongue will be accepted and understood in your country or place of destination. Or, to put it another way, not bothering to learn the lingo for your trip.

It doesn't take too much effort to learn, at the very least, 'hello' and 'thank you', and chances are your efforts will be received with gratitude. It doesn't matter if you've just ordered a pink hippo instead of a ham and cheese croissant, your waiter will thank you for trying!

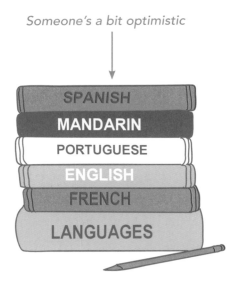

Someone's a bit optimistic

FINAL WORD

You are now officially travel-hack-ready! You can go anywhere at any time, safe in the knowledge that you can pack like a pro, find the best deal on your flight and comfortably survive everything from interminable car journeys to danger in the great outdoors. Happy hacking!

HACKS INDEX

IMAGE CREDITS

Illustrations within the book were inspired by the following people's photographs.

STUDENT HACKS

Tips and Tricks to Make Uni Life Easier

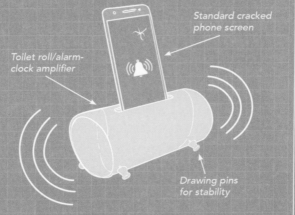

Standard cracked phone screen

Toilet roll/alarm-clock amplifier

Drawing pins for stability

Dan Marshall

Over **130** amazing hacks inside!

STUDENT HACKS

Tips and Tricks to Make Uni Life Easier

Dan Marshall

ISBN: 978 1 78685 246 5

£9.99

Paperback

Do you struggle to get out of bed for class in the morning?

Do you become enraged when your beer bottles topple over in the fridge?

Have you ever wished you could listen to your lectures in half the time?

This fully illustrated manual solves your everyday dilemmas, from ways to make your student loan stretch further to revision hacks and much, much more. Whether you're a fresh-faced fresher or a seasoned student searching for shortcuts, this trusty guide will make your uni life easier, more productive and, most importantly, more fun.

THE
BACKPACKER'S
SURVIVAL
GUIDE

 EVERYTHING

you need

 to KNOW

Tamsin King